Augustus

"And . . . there went out a decree from Caesar Augustus, that all the world should be taxed." (Luke 2:1)

Tiberius

"In the fifteenth year of the reign of Tiberius Caesar . . . the word of God came unto John . . . in the wilderness." (Luke 3:1, 2)

Claudius

"Claudius had commanded all Jews to depart from Rome." (Acts 18:2)

Nero

"Then said Paul, . . . I appeal unto Caesar. Then Festus answered, . . . unto Caesar shalt thou go." (Acts 25:10–12)

COINS OF THE NEW TESTAMENT PERIOD PORTRAYING ROMAN EMPERORS NAMED IN THE BIBLE

COINS
OF
BIBLE DAYS

by

FLORENCE AIKEN BANKS

Sanford J. Durst
Numismatic Publications
New York, N.Y.

FOREWORD

The Judeo-Christian Foundation of Western World religious traditions constantly seeks new evidence of its foundation.

Coinage is probably one of the best areas providing such evidence. Numerous authors and historians over the past century have contributed to the literature, among them Madden, Hill and more recently Meshorer, Kindler, Hendin, Yoeman and Klawans, among others.

Florence Aiken Banks' effort, this book, ranks high in the quality literature available on the subject of the economics and monetary matters of the biblical period. She provides an excellent insight of the historical significance of that early coinage. As a publisher of a large number of numismatic titles, I can advise that one of the most often asked for books is this volume, which has been out of print for quite some time.

As a collector of ancient coinage of the biblical period, I recommend the hobby highly as an enjoyable, and educational pastime. To those who partake, and to those who merely wish to acquaint themselves with the subject, even on a superficial basis, I recommend this volume.

Numismatically yours,

Sanford J. Durst
President
FOUNDATION FOR NUMISMATIC
EDUCATION, INC.

Dedicated
in loving remembrance
to my foster mother
DEE E. AIKEN
(MRS. JOHN C. AIKEN)

Introduction and Acknowledgments

When I was a child my parents had two friends, both bishops, who were enthusiastic travelers in Bible lands. Whenever they returned to this country's Pacific Coast they came to my parents' home. How I did wrap myself in the stories of some of the articles they brought from the Holy Land! Would I ever set *my* foot where Jesus had walked? Would I ever hold in *my* hand something Jesus had known?

After I had grown up I stood, in Rome, at the stair down which Jesus had walked when he went out of Pilate's Judgment Hall. I could not become so elated as I had thought I would be should I ever know a spot where Jesus had trod. Somehow the thought would keep coming: "Yes, it is the stair which Jesus descended, but it is not where it was when he was on it." Then would come the question: *"Where* could I stand on the same footing as that on which Jesus stood? By the well of Sychar? Yes and no, for in the course of nineteen hundred years the soil by that well has changed completely. Possibly on the bridge at Caesarea Philippi? I wonder!"

On I would go with that absorbing desire to come in contact with things that Jesus had touched. It was a childhood fancy I never could outgrow.

Then one day in the 1930's there came into my hands a certain coin. I told myself there could be no doubt that

Jesus had handled others like it, and perhaps, yes, perhaps it was possible . . .

And so I held on to the same early childhood desire to touch something Jesus had touched. That is the story of how nearly twenty years ago I began the gathering of *Coins of Bible Days*. I wrote story after story of these coins, and in November of 1950 these accounts began to appear regularly in the numismatic paper *Kelly's Coins and Chatter*. Such stories in a periodical require presentation in a form which would not be suitable for a book, yet I felt that they contained material which might be worth preserving in more lasting form, so I gathered them together with the idea of making a book of them.

After I had done this, however, I realized that I had been too many years at the searching out of those coins; the whole manuscript needed revising. Moreover, archaeologists had discovered facts that seventeen or even ten years ago I could not have known. Plainly, the task of complete revision was before me.

Then I had the good fortune to learn of Frances Williams Browin of Philadelphia and of her exceptional ability in that line. Yes, it would be a tremendous task, but she was willing to undertake it.

On picking up the first draft of her revision and finding the book opening with a story I had placed in the middle of my manuscript, I began to realize what an improvement her editing could make. Mrs. Browin has done a splendid piece of rewriting, and my deep gratitude goes to her.

Both Mrs. Browin and I are grateful to Miss Dorothy H. Cox of the University Museum, Philadelphia, for her invaluable assistance in verifying coin attributions, translating legends, and checking technical numismatic details.

A word of appreciation is due the artist, David Bowers, for his painstaking care and skill in preparing the endpaper map.

I owe my thanks to Sid Fredrickson of Roseburg, Oregon, for his earnest endeavor to make the best possible photographs of the coins I have gathered together. Such photographs are important to me not only as illustrations for this book, but also because they make it possible for me to examine at any time the likenesses of the coins themselves, which naturally I do not keep in my home. I am also indebted to the American Numismatic Society's New York headquarters for furnishing photographs of a number of significant coins which I was not fortunate enough to have in my own collection. Because all illustrations show coins in their actual size the use of a magnifying glass is frequently necessary for the deciphering of details.

FLORENCE AIKEN BANKS

Roseburg, Oregon
May, 1955

Contents

(Coin illustrations in every case pertain to the chapter that follows)

Seeing the Past Through Coins

The handling of ancient coins does with time what radio, television, and airplanes do with space. Carry a few tetra-drachms and farthings in your pocket, and somehow you will find the world of two thousand or more years ago moving up to yesterday.

Not only the earnest student of the Bible but even the sophisticate who scoffs at Biblical history cannot help feeling a genuine thrill when he discovers that he himself may actually see and feel the very bits of silver, bronze, and gold which served for the peoples of that distant day precisely the same purposes that our dimes and dollars serve for us.

When we hold in our palms.the one thing we *can* hold which we have a reasonable right to believe could have been in the hand of Nicodemus when he bought the hundred pounds of myrrh and aloes for Jesus' burial, in the hand of Martha when she went to market, in the hand of Mary of Bethany when she bought her precious alabaster box of spikenard, or in the money bag of Judas when he purchased food for the Disciples, we feel a closer acquaintance with those personages of the Bible than we had ever dreamed we could.

Coins of the Biblical era were not called in for frequent replacements, as are our coins today. For hundreds of years they remained in circulation—or rather they remained in circulation unless they happened to be hidden away or buried, as frequently they were. Ancient peoples were great hoarders. Having no banks in which to deposit their precious earnings, they hid money, of necessity, in walls, in caves, and in the ground. Hardly a week passes but that some hitherto unsuspected deposit of this money is dug up.

There is, moreover, a whole busy field of archaeology devoted entirely to recovering the cargoes of ships which sank millenniums ago. The Mediterranean seafarers and traders, in their comparatively flimsy vessels, were at the mercy of storms and suffered many shipwrecks. Among the relics of such wrecks which divers now are bringing to light are quantities of ancient coins, each one with its story to tell of a world which is vanished.

Because of frequent discoveries of such treasure troves, the coins of ancient Greece and Rome and their contemporaries are not nearly so scarce as might be expected. In fact, some of them are more plentiful than are the coins of the infant United States issued in the late eighteenth century. Nor is the price of these heritages from Biblical times so high (with certain exceptions) as to discourage people in moderate circumstances from becoming collectors. If you can buy a drachma or a lepton or a denarius two thousand years old for no more than it would cost to go to a movie, why not buy the coin and enjoy the lasting sense of contact it gives you with those long-gone ancestors from whom our religions and our civilization have sprung?

One of the purposes of this book is to show how these ancient coins serve as confirmation for many parts of the Bible. Perhaps more graphically and more tangibly than any other medium available, these moneys of the past can help us in mapping a path of accord between Biblical and secular history. It is true that the Bible itself mentions comparatively few coins, yet many pieces struck between the eighth century B.C. (when coinage began) and the early Christian era are deeply imbued with Biblical associations. In short, Biblical history is *in* them—an inseparable part of them. And—wonder of wonders—many of them are still available today for us to study and enjoy!

Although the study of coins is a highly specialized field, one need not be a serious numismatist or even an embryo numismatist in order to derive real pleasure and profit from contemplation of the coins of Bible days and of the stories which they have to tell. Like all sciences, numismatics has a vocabulary all its own; but this volume purposely avoids any numismatic patter which is not intelligible to the layman. All that the reader needs to know about coins is that the more important side is the *obverse,* the less important side is the *reverse,* the portion between the design and the coin's edge is the *field,* and the words in the field are the *legend.* Any other out-of-the-ordinary words which may creep in from time to time may be found in the Glossary.

And now, before moving on to a consideration of the coins known to the world of the Bible, we must let ourselves be carried back briefly to an even more ancient era: that today almost unimaginable world in which the very concept of coins as a medium of exchange had not yet been devised.

2

Before Coins

The first wealthy man of whom the Bible tells was Abraham, but because he lived in the nineteenth century B.C. he never had the fun of jingling coins in his pocket, even though he "was very rich in cattle, in silver, and in gold." [1] Not until more than a thousand years after Abraham's day, in fact, did the first coins appear.

On ordinary occasions Abraham's pocket was an adjunct to his girdle, but because the granules and ingots of silver and gold which he used as his medium of exchange were extremely heavy he or his servants doubtless had to carry special bags filled with these precious metals whenever he was contemplating any major financial transactions. Certainly he must always have needed to have with him a small set of scales or weights to aid him in his dealings. This we know because of the description in Genesis of his negotiations when, after the death of Sarah, his wife, he asked the sons of Heth in the Land of Canaan to "intreat for me to Ephron the son of Zohar, that he may give me the cave of Machpelah . . . for as much money as it is worth he shall give it me for a possession of a buryingplace amongst you. . . . And Ephron answered Abraham, saying . . . the land is worth four hundred shekels of silver. . . . And Abraham . . . weighed to Ephron . . . four hundred shekels of silver. . . .

[1] Genesis 13:2. All Biblical quotations throughout this book are from the King James Version.

5

And after this, Abraham buried Sarah his wife in the cave of the field of Machpelah." [2]

Thus we find that the silver shekel was originally not a coin, but a measure of weight. It was roughly equivalent to one and a half ounces avoirdupois in our scale of weights. The silver shekel's value varied slightly from time to time and from place to place, but as accurate as possible an estimate of its worth in Abraham's era is 54.74 cents in American money. This means that the Bible's first rich man weighed on his scale and turned over to Ephron about thirty-seven and a half pounds of silver valued at approximately $218.96 in order to acquire as a burial place for his wife the cave of the field of Machpelah where eventually he himself too was interred, as were Isaac, Rebekah, Leah, and Jacob. [3] Abraham's silver shekels are long scattered, but the burial cave which he purchased is there today for all to see.

It is ironic that Abraham and his family should have had to find their final resting place in Canaan, for, as a native of Ur of the Chaldees, Abraham always felt that Canaan was a strange and foreign land. That is why, when the time came for his son Isaac to marry, the old man dreaded the possibility of having a Canaanite for a daughter-in-law, and accordingly sent his most trusted servant back to Haran in Mesopotamia, to his own and Sarah's people, to find a wife for Isaac.

No one who has read the Bible needs to be reminded of how the old servant found Rebekah, the ideal wife for Isaac, when she brought her pitcher to the well just outside Haran. Not only was "the damsel . . . very fair to look upon," but she showed herself to be thoughtful and generous. Best of all, she proved to be a granddaughter of

[2] *Ibid.*, 23:2–19.
[3] *Ibid.*, 49:29–31 and 50:13.

Abraham's brother Nahor, so the servant lost no time in winning her favor by giving her presents—"a golden earring of half a shekel weight, and two bracelets for her hands of ten shekels weight of gold." With these and other gifts of "jewels of silver and jewels of gold," and with his moving tale of how the Lord had ordained his choice, he persuaded Rebekah to leave her home in Haran and go with him to Canaan to become Isaac's wife (and, in due course, the mother of Biblical history's first twins, Jacob and Esau). [4]

Jewelry served very effectively in place of money to negotiate a bargain; in fact, it was made in certain specific weights so that it would be convenient, when necessary, as a sort of coinage. But it should be noted that the half-shekel golden earring and the ten-shekel golden bracelets which first captured Rebekah's interest were worth far more than if they had been of silver. The ratio of value between gold and silver was roughly 16 to 1, which meant that a shekel of gold was worth about $8.76 as compared with the silver shekel's 54.74 cents. The gold in Rebekah's engagement-gift earring, therefore, may be valued in our currency at about $4.38; that in her bracelets at $87.60.

For sealing a matrimonial arrangement this may not have been a great deal of money, but it was a vast sum indeed compared to the "twenty pieces of silver" [5] for which, years later (about 1729 B.C.), nine of Rebekah's and Isaac's grandsons (the sons of Jacob, later known as Israel) basely sold into slavery their next-to-youngest brother, Joseph, simply because they were jealous of him and wished to be rid of him.

Joseph's purchasers—Midianite traders on their way to Egypt—paid for their human merchandise with Egyptian money, which is thought to have been flat rings of silver;

[4] *Ibid.*, 24:15–53 and 25:21–26.
[5] *Ibid.*, 37:28.

in terms of modern United States currency Joseph was sold
for about $10.95. If this money was divided equally among
nine of Joseph's ten older brothers (omitting Reuben, who
tried to save the boy and hence presumably did not share
in the booty), it seems fair to assume that for this nefarious
bargain each of the brothers received the Egyptian equivalent of slightly less than $1.25 in United States money. A
dollar and a quarter apiece for selling the wealthy Abraham's great-grandson into bondage!

It is a long way, both in time and in monetary value,
from the sordid occasion of Joseph's betrayal to the great
days over three centuries later when the twelve tribes of
Israel—descendants of that same Joseph and his erstwhile
erring brethren—tendered the vast offerings of valued goods
which enabled them to furnish their long-awaited tabernacle in the Promised Land.

This mammoth example of pre-coinage evaluation had
its start in or about 1491 B.C. when Moses, leading the
Children of Israel on their epic journey from Egypt to the
Valley of the Jordan, received at Mount Sinai the divine
instructions for the tabernacle's furnishings. Here, for the
first time in the Bible, we find mention of that precious
weight, the golden talent. "And thou shalt make a candlestick of pure gold. . . ." the Lord told Moses. "Of a talent
of pure gold . . ." [6]

A talent of pure gold! How much would that be worth
in terms of American money? A tremendous amount for a
candlestick and its appurtenances, even by modern standards, for most authorities are agreed that the golden talent
(weighing somewhere between 57 and 95 pounds) was
worth $26,280—sixteen times as much as a silver talent,
3,000 times as much as a golden shekel, 48,000 times as
much as a silver shekel!

[6] Exodus 25:31 and 39.

This massive candlestick, with its carefully prescribed accessories, was only one of the many costly offerings (enumerated in precise detail in Numbers 7) with which, within the next year, the beloved tabernacle was equipped. The chronicler is meticulous in estimating the metallic value of the sundry contributions of each of the heads of the twelve tribes. From Nahshon of the tribe of Judah— Nahshon, the ancestor of Jesus—there was "one silver charger, the weight thereof was an hundred and thirty shekels, one silver bowl of seventy shekels . . . one spoon of ten shekels of gold. . . ." [7]

And so it went on, with similar offerings from the tribe of Issachar, the tribe of Zebulun, and all the rest, until, on the day when the great altar at last was anointed and dedicated, there were twenty-four silver vessels weighing, in all, 2,400 shekels, and twelve golden spoons weighing 120 shekels. With silver shekels valued at 54.74 cents and gold shekels at $8.76, these contributions were worth, in our money, $1,313.76 for the former and $1,051.20 for the latter—small change, perhaps, compared to the fabulous $26,280 candlestick, and yet representing no mean sacrifice for the Children of Israel in those days when they still were hard-pressed.

No wonder, then, that centuries later a series of foreign invaders, on capturing Jerusalem, pounced with especial glee upon the treasured utensils of silver and gold which they found in the tabernacle. Among these invaders were the Romans who went so far as to record, for all posterity to see, the story of their plunder! High on the huge Arch of Titus on the Via Sacra in Rome there appears unto this day the carven scene of the captive Jews being forced by their conquerors to strip their temple of all its precious furnishings. Whether the candlestick made "of a talent of

[7] Numbers 7:12–14.

pure gold" was included in the Roman loot or whether it already had fallen into the hands of earlier conquerors we never can hope to know.

By the time the Romans arrived, the talent's weight and the shekel's weight had given way to coins as mediums of value and exchange, but in the years before that revolutionary change took place we find recorded in the Bible the account of a certain financial transaction which should be of great comfort to any modern reader who is concerned about the high cost of present-day medical care.

The story is that of Naaman, captain of the host of the King of Syria in the year 895 B.C. Naaman "was a great man with his master . . . but he was a leper." Leprosy, of course, was deemed incurable, but a captive Israelite slave girl serving as maid to Naaman's wife told her mistress that she was sure her husband could be healed of his malady if he would go to Samaria to be ministered to by the Israelite prophet Elisha.

Soon word of the slave girl's remark reached the king, who promptly told Naaman: "Go to, go, and I will send a letter unto the king of Israel. And he departed, and took with him ten talents of silver, and six thousand pieces of gold." [8]

Ten talents of silver and 6,000 pieces of gold—this is the price which the King of Syria was willing to pay to have the captain of his host delivered from leprosy! All in all this was quite a sum, for the silver talents, at $1,642.50 apiece, would be worth $16,425, and the 6,000 pieces of gold, believed to be gold shekel weights worth $8.76 apiece, would come to $52,560, making the total of silver and gold $68,985—an impressive fee in any age for even a major medical miracle, and an impressive weight, as well, for Naaman and his servants to carry on their journey. Accord-

[8] II Kings 5:1–16.

ing to the most conservative estimates the ten talents of silver would have weighed about 600 pounds and the 6,000 gold shekels about 200 pounds; but they very possibly may have been far heavier, for authorities never have agreed concerning this matter of Biblical weights. In any case, it was a sizable load.

Elisha, as every Bible reader knows, turned out to be quite worthy of the reputation for wonder-working which the slave girl had given him: not only did he cleanse Naaman of his leprosy by having him bathe seven times in the waters of the Jordan, but—nearly as great a wonder— he refused to accept any part of the $68,985 fee which the Syrian captain proffered him! Therefore Naaman and his retinue returned to their own country still loaded with the weight of all that treasure of gold and silver—or all, to be precise, except for two talents' weight of silver which Elisha's servant Gehazi got from the Syrian by chicanery.

It is worthy of note that the two talents alone which Gehazi tried to misappropriate (less than 5 per cent of the total fee offered) were heavy enough to need two servants to carry them. [9] In short, it was a burdensome, generally impracticable business to carry about enough gold and silver to make financial transactions, according to the ancient formula of payment in terms of weight. The time was ripe for the development of some new medium of exchange which would do away forever with this cumbersome code of values.

That time was not long in arriving; it came (though not, to be sure, for the Israelites) less than a century after Elisha's miraculous cure of Naaman the leper.

[9] *Ibid.*, 5:23.

LYDIA: One-third stater of the time of Alyattes (father of Croesus), 617–560 B.C. The coin is made of electrum, an alloy of silver and gold. The obverse shows a lion's head; the reverse shows only the incuse.

LYDIA: Gold or silver stater of the time of Croesus, 560–546 B.C. The foreparts of a lion and of a bull face each other on the obverse. Two rectangular incuse punches mark the reverse.

PERSIA: Gold daric of a type struck by Persia's kings for two centuries, beginning with latter part of the sixth century B.C. The king on the obverse, half kneeling, holds a bow and a spear. The reverse shows an oblong incuse punch. Silver sigloi of the same period were almost precisely similar in appearance.

3

Pioneers of Coinage

Because the Hebrews, around whose history and philosophy the Old Testament is built, were not among the first makers or the first users of coins, we have to wander somewhat afield in order to trace the genesis of those early coins which the persons who play a part in Bible history must have used in increasing numbers as the years went by.

It is true that the Hebrews were in the main a pastoral people and, like all pastoral people of their era and even of some sections of the world today, generally conducted their trade on a basis of barter, using sheep or cows as a standard of value. (So common and widespread was this practice that the Roman word for money, *pecunia,* was derived from *pecus,* the Latin word for cattle.) Yet sheep and cows were far from satisfactory as a portable, flexible means of exchange, and even the measuring of value by a system of weights in gold and silver was, as we have seen, an awkward method with grave defects.

Practically all historians and numismatists agree that the very earliest coins probably were made about seven centuries before Christ in the kingdom of Lydia, and that these were followed soon after by the silver turtle-pieces of the small Greek island-city of Aegina. Whether any of these were the first money known to the Hebrews is doubtful, for we have no specific record of the Bible's people coming into contact with the Lydian or Greek coins of this era;

whereas, scourged as they were by the Assyrians, it is
entirely possible that they may have seen some of the Assyrians' cast half-shekel pieces. Admittedly this is only
guesswork, for none of those half-shekel pieces ever have
been found; and the only basis for believing that they
actually existed is the reference that Sennacherib, the Assyrian emperor, made to them at almost the exact time
(701–690 B.C.) when he and his armies were laying Palestine to waste and besieging Jerusalem in the period of
King Hezekiah and the prophet Isaiah. [1]

Discounting the faint possibility that the Hebrews may
have known those almost mythical Assyrian coins, we can
move onto surer ground and say with certainty that they
were very closely acquainted with Persian coinage of the
sixth century B.C. Without doubt these were the first coins
which the characters of Biblical narrative really used and
handled to any marked extent. Ample record of their
familiarity with Persian money is supplied not only by the
Bible but by many chronicles of secular history.

How the Jews' introduction to Persian coins came about
is a fairly complicated story of a series of armed conquests.
It all began (as mentioned above) with Lydia, which lay
along what is now the coast of Turkey east of the Aegean
Sea in western Asia Minor. Lydia's inhabitants possessed
a highly developed commercial civilization. Her kings were
fabulously rich, deriving much of their wealth from their
country's abundant natural resources of gold and silver.
At some time very close to 700 B.C., one of these wealthy
Lydian rulers devised the idea of cutting precious metal
into small convenient lumps of a fixed weight and then of
stamping these lumps with official symbols to indicate that
the state guaranteed their value. These pieces of Lydian

[1] James Henry Breasted, *The Conquest of Civilization* (New York, Harper &
Brothers, 1938), p. 156.

money are commonly recognized as "the world's first coins."

Just which one of two or three Lydian coins was the very earliest of all is not definitely known. Often credited with that honor is one of electrum (a pale yellow alloy of gold and silver) with a side-angled view of a lion's head on its obverse and nothing on its reverse but the scar of the moneyer's punch. Lucky is the rare collector who possesses one of these!

Possibly the tiny one-third stater of King Alyattes pictured here may be one of these very earliest of coins; but whether or not it can claim this honor it most assuredly bears a close resemblance to that almost legendary "first," for in ancient days a piece of money was kept in service for scores of years and sometimes even for centuries after it was issued, without any change being made in its design (called "type" by numismatists). And because these earliest coins bore no legends, it is practically impossible to date them accurately.

Rich though Lydia was in gold (we are told that the sands of the little Pactolus River flowing through Sardis, the magnificent capital city, were literally "golden sands"), [2] more than a century passed between the production of those original electrum pieces and the issuing of the first coins of pure gold. This pioneer gold coinage came into being, fittingly enough, during the reign of Croesus, whose name has come down to us as a synonym for extreme wealth. From 560 to 546 B.C., during Croesus' reign, the kingdom of Lydia put out some little gold coins which may still be seen, though they are extremely rare and extremely precious. Numismatists call them, together with their silver counterparts, "Lydian staters" or "staters of Croesus."

The moneyers of Croesus' time, like those of his predecessors, chose to mark their coinage with animal symbols. On

[2] *The Columbia Encyclopedia.*

the obverse of these staters of Croesus appears not just one animal's head, but two: a lion with wide-open mouth confronting, on the right, a horned bull. On the reverse are two stamped-in rectangles ("incuse squares," we call them), usually unequal in size. The silver staters are precisely like the gold ones in appearance, but their value in terms of Lydian coinage was only one-tenth as much. This 10-to-1 ratio between gold and silver, introduced by Croesus, is perhaps a reflection of the abundance of gold in Lydia, for it is a much smaller evaluation of gold in terms of silver than we usually find either in ancient or in modern coinage.

Perhaps it would be well to qualify the statement made above that "silver staters are precisely like the gold ones in appearance." That is not strictly true; as a matter of fact no two ancient coins are *precisely* alike. In size and shape they vary greatly, for the coinmaker used no collar to keep the planchet or lump of metal from spreading when he struck the punch with his mallet; therefore sometimes Lydian staters were only a half-inch in diameter (like the one illustrated here) and at other times a full three-quarter inch across. The result depended on the softness of the metal and on how much hammering the moneyer did. Though the official stamp was a guarantee of the *quality* of the metal, it could not be a guarantee of its exact weight.

It seems almost incredible that these tiny staters should have survived for more than twenty-five hundred years. No wonder that the mere sight and touch of them, weaving as they do an unbroken thread of continuity between our day and the pomp and mystery of a long-vanished era, have been known to cause even the most hardened of scoffers to yield to the temptation to become collectors! It is ironic to reflect, certainly, on how very much greater have been the powers of survival of these mere bits of metal than were those of the storied monarch who created them. For Croesus, deluded by his wealth into believing that he and his nation were invincible, made the mistake, about 549 B.C., of venturing into a trial of arms with the mighty Cyrus, King of Persia, and within two years that foolhardy venture brought the end not only of Croesus' kingship and his fabulous wealth but also of Lydia's existence as an independent nation.

Cyrus and his Persian army were not forces to be trifled with. Five or six years before the conquest of Lydia this first of the great Persian emperors, rebelling against the rule of the Medes, his neighbors to the north in the mountains east of the Tigris, had overthrown Media and united that country with Persia to create the Persian Empire—an empire far more powerful than any preceding it. Having now taken Lydia too in his stride, the victorious Cyrus moved on within the next decade to capture Babylon as well. And it was in Babylon that his path crossed that of the Jews and made its mark on Biblical history.

For the Jews, as every Bible student knows, had been unhappy captives in Babylon for nearly fifty years, ever since Nebuchadnezzar had reduced Jerusalem to ruins in 586 B.C. as a grim lesson to its inhabitants, who had revolted against his eleven-year dominion. In their enforced exile the Jews were unwilling witnesses to the series of feats through which Nebuchadnezzar, as emperor, made Babylon the greatest city of the ancient world; indeed, some of them, like Daniel (who became a great favorite with Nebuchadnezzar), fared rather well in their captivity; but through it all they had but one desire, one obsession: to return to their homeland. It was in the midst of this prevalent mood of desperate longing on the part of the captive people that Belshazzar, Nebuchadnezzar's successor, held his famous feast at which appeared the handwriting on the wall.

Down through the ages the story of that superhuman

handwriting has been told and retold: how the emperor, beholding the cryptic words "MENE, MENE, TEKEL, UPHARSIN" inscribed upon the wall of the banquet hall by a disembodied Hand, was mystified and struck with terror; how the Jewish captive Daniel explained the meaning of the words ("God hath numbered thy kingdom, and finished it. . . . Thou are weighed in the balances, and art found wanting. . . . Thy kingdom is divided, and given to the Medes and Persians"); and how Belshazzar was slain that very night. [3]

Here we strike a slight snag, for Daniel now relates that "Darius the Median took the kingdom, being about threescore and two years old," [4] whereas from all available records of secular history we know that it was not Darius, but Cyrus, who conquered Babylon in 538 B.C. Cyrus did not die until 529 B.C., nine years after this conquest, and Darius the Great did not become ruler of the Persian Empire until 521, eight years after Cyrus's death. The Bible's crediting of the overthrow of Babylon to the second of the outstanding Persian emperors instead of to the first was probably only a slip of the pen, such as all scribes, modern as well as ancient, are likely to make from time to time; obviously Cyrus, not Darius, must have been meant, for sixty-two is the age which Cyrus had reached in the year 538.

Whatever the momentary lapse of the chronicler of Daniel, there can be no doubt that the coming of the Persian emperor to Babylon was the deliverance for which the long-captive Jews had been praying. It was the very deliverance, indeed, which—more than a century before Cyrus was born—Isaiah had prophesied when he said: "I am the Lord that . . . saith of Cyrus, He is my shepherd,

[3] Daniel 5:25–30.
[4] *Ibid.*, 5:31.

and shall perform all my pleasure: even saying to Jerusalem, Thou shalt be built; and to the temple, Thy foundation shall be laid." [5] The exiles promptly greeted the new
ruler as their liberator, and Cyrus justified their faith by
releasing them from thralldom and allowing them to return
to their native land, where he aided them in getting re-
settled, perhaps in the belief that they would serve as a
buffer between his empire and Egypt.

When the Hebrews returned to Jerusalem in 536 B.C.,
they carried with them something which they had not had
when they went into exile half a century before: vast quantities of Persian coins. For these they were indirectly indebted to the vanquished kingdom of Lydia, for Cyrus had
had no coinage before his conquest of Croesus, but had
been quick to adopt this wonderful idea as soon as the
Lydian mint at Sardis fell into his hands. Lydia's practiced
moneyers were promptly put to work at making coins for
Persia's far-flung empire, and a generous share of these
flowed into the newly annexed land of Babylon; from there,
naturally enough, they accompanied the Jews on their
homeward trek to Jerusalem.

The Persian coinage consisted of gold darics (also called
drams) and silver sigloi. (Possibly the darics got their name
from Darius the Great, who in due course followed Cyrus
to the emperor's throne.) Following the precedent set by
the Lydian staters on which they were modeled, these
golden darics and silver sigloi were precisely alike in appearance, although they differed greatly in their value—
differed far more, in fact, than did their Lydian prototypes,
the Persian gold-silver ratio being 20-to-1 in place of the
Lydian 10-to-1. In so far as it is possible to make any statement as to the value of ancient coins in terms of modern
money, it may be said that a siglos was equivalent to about

[5] Isaiah 44:24 and 28.

27 cents and a dram or daric to $5.40. All such attempted evaluations as these are bound to be misleading, however, for actually the money of another era can be valued for us only in terms of the commodities it would buy.

The design of these early Persian coins is a marked change from that of the Lydian ones. In place of the animals which Croesus and his predecessors favored, Cyrus and Darius chose to present the likeness of a king. On darics and sigloi alike we find a lively image of a crowned royal personage kneeling in battle. In his left hand he carries a drawn bow and in his right a spear, while across his back is flung a quiver full of arrows. On the reverse is only the incuse: a single oblong, as compared with the pair of near squares on Lydia's staters.

That many of these Persian coins or their predecessors were in the Jews' possession when they returned to their Holy City is not mere conjecture; it is definitely stated in the Bible. There was, for instance, the first caravan, led by Zerubbabel, of which Ezra says: "And some of the chief of the fathers, when they came to the house of the Lord which is at Jerusalem, offered freely for the house of God . . . three-score and one thousand drams. . . ." [6] These are the first coins to be mentioned in the Bible.

With the dram (or daric) valued at $5.40, this means that Zerubbabel's caravan contributed $5,724 toward the rebuilding of the temple which Nebuchadnezzar had destroyed fifty years before. Later on, the second caravan (of which Ezra himself was a part) brought "twenty basons of gold, of a thousand drams. . . ." [7] It is significant that although this was a gift of goods, not money ("basons" being the spelling for "basins" in the period of King James's scriveners), the Hebrews had by now become so familiar

[6] Ezra 2:68, 69.
[7] *Ibid.*, 8:27.

with the use and convenience of coinage that they enumerated almost everything, as we do today, in terms of money value.

From then on the gifts to the treasure in the temple are consistently recorded not in talents and shekels, as had been done in earlier days, but in drams. In fact, in the space of just three verses of Nehemiah we find contributions of 41,000 golden drams reported, plus great quantities of silver. [8] That means nearly a quarter of a million dollars in our terms!

The use of coins was here to stay among the Israelites, as elsewhere.

[8] Nehemiah 7:70–72.

AEGINA: Silver stater, about 650–600 B.C., with a sea turtle on the obverse and with an incuse of mill sail (windmill) pattern on the reverse.

AEGINA: Silver stater, about 480–431 B.C. The earlier crude sea turtle has been markedly improved; the incuse now has five uneven compartments.

AKRAGAS (now Agrigento in Sicily): Silver didrachm, about 550–472 B.C. The eagle on the obverse was an emblem of Zeus; the crab on the reverse was possibly a badge of the city.

METAPONTUM (Greek colony in Lucania, now southern Italy): Silver stater, about 550–470 B.C., featuring an ear of barley on both faces.

DYRRHACHIUM (colony of Corinth on western Adriatic coast): Silver stater, about 450–350 B.C. The obverse shows a cow suckling a calf; a formal decorative pattern is on the reverse.

THEBES (as head of Boeotian League): Silver stater, about 379–338 B.C. The obverse bears a Boeotian shield and the reverse an amphora (wine jug), flanked by the letters of the magistrate's name in abbreviated form.

ATHENS: Silver tetradrachm, about 480 B.C. The head of Athena fills the entire field on the obverse. The reverse shows Athena's owl and olive branch (sacred to her), together with the name of the city, abbreviated.

ELIS: Silver drachm, about 370–362 B.C. The head of Zeus on the obverse is now almost obliterated, but the eagle and thunderbolt (emblems of Zeus) are still clear on the concave reverse.

CORINTH: Silver didrachm, fourth century B.C. This is unusual in that Pegasus appears on the obverse, while the head of Athena, found on the obverse of most coins, is here on the reverse. She wears a Corinthian helmet. In the right field is a magistrate's symbol: Artemis running, holding a torch.

26

4

The Pervasive Greeks

Although Palestine did not actually fall under Greek rule until about 333 B.C., the heyday of Alexander the Great, it could not escape the far-reaching Greek influence which during this period gradually stamped the Hellenic pattern, in varying degrees, upon the whole Mediterranean world. It is true that, for the more than two centuries between their return to Palestine and Alexander's conquest, the Jews lived and thrived under the nominal rule of Persian emperors who granted to the Hebrew governors wide latitude to do what seemed best for their people and their religion. Yet all the while the subtle sway of Greece and the Greeks was growing.

What *were* the Greeks, exactly? That is a hard question, for they were never a closely united people in the sense in which a modern nation is united. They were, rather, the widely scattered heirs to the ancient Aegean civilization of Homeric and pre-Homeric times, held loosely together by a common language, a common script, a common background of epic and religious myths, and a shared interest in commerce, sports, and culture. Tireless wanderers, they permeated region after region, until by the middle of the sixth century B.C. they were well entrenched in numerous strategic spots along the Mediterranean and the Black Sea, having attained these footholds more through trade and industry than through force of arms. Many of their outposts were small city-states or islands which, though nominally independent, considered themselves Greek quite as much as if they had been bound to Athens by a strong central rule.

In all the many lands to which the Jews dispersed at the time of the successive invasions which ravaged their homeland, the Greeks were firmly established, while around Judea itself there was a wide scattering of Greek settlements and cities, each with its characteristically Greek institutions. From these settlements Greek traders and other travelers came to Jerusalem, bringing with them not only their coins but also many other aspects of a civilization vastly different from that of the predominantly agricultural, puritanical, God-fearing Jews.

The contrast between the two was enormous in many fields, and in religion it was especially marked. Religion was the primary basis of the Hebrews' life; scorning idolatry, they held fast (with occasional backslidings, to be sure) to a strictly ordered belief in one God and to a persistent dream of righteousness. For the Greeks, however, the gods were merely glorified human beings of heroic size, whom they looked upon with little awe and with a tolerant amusement at their all-too-human vices. They had no equivalent for the Jewish idea of a solemn, omnipotent Lord of all creation.

To the Bible student, be he Christian or Jewish, the Greeks' tongue-in-cheek attitude toward a multitude of gods may seem superstitious and childish, yet familiarity with Greco-Roman mythology is highly necessary for anyone who wishes to understand just what kind of religion Luke and Paul and the other early Christian missionaries had to overcome. This is one of the reasons why the collecting and study of old Greek coins holds so much fascination, for these coins, bearing, as many of them do, the images of major and minor gods and goddesses, are concrete, visible proof that the ancient mythology of which we all have heard was once an active, potent force in the world of every day—even in the world of Jews who worshiped one Supreme Being.

The mythical residents of Mount Olympus did not hold exclusive sway over Greek coinage, for in the early days (as the accompanying photographs show) there were a number of simple designs showing such everyday objects as wine jugs, shields, and grain, and animals such as cattle, birds, and turtles. It is not surprising that the first Greeks to make coins should have used animals for their themes, as did the pioneer moneyers of Lydia, for the earliest Greek coins of which we know—those of Aegina—were made almost immediately after those historic, animal-conscious Lydian pieces which were the forerunners of all coinage. Aegina in those days ranked ahead of Athens (about twenty miles to its eastward) in commercial importance. Being an island, it was naturally a maritime state, and many of its mariners must have visited the ports of Lydia in their trading expeditions across the Aegean Sea. From such contacts came an early acquaintance with that outstanding Lydian invention: coinage.

It is true that the Aeginetans, like the Lydians, stamped their first coins (made at the very beginning of the seventh century B.C.) with the likenesses of animals, but what a difference there was in the animals they selected for this purpose! In place of the kingly, roaring lion of Lydia there appeared on Aegina's silver coins the humble turtle—symbolic, no doubt, of the Aeginetans' seafaring nature. There are some students of ancient numismatics, however, who believe that the turtle was placed on the Aeginetan stater not merely as a maritime symbol but also as a token of honor to Aphrodite, the Greek goddess of beauty and love who, according to legend, originally had sprung from the foam of the sea.

Whatever the turtle's significance may have been, it is certain that those pioneer Greek coins were not round, as are our coins today, but were shaped like teardrops. In thickness, too, they were at the outset very irregular. The turtle which they bore had a smooth coat, marked on its back (if time has not eroded the markings) with six tiny buttons.

As time went on, the shape and appearance of Aegina's silver money steadily improved, but for nearly two hundred years there was but one theme for the design: the turtle. True, the turtle changed materially in appearance, evolving gradually from a creature of the sea to a land tortoise with thirteen shingles for a roof—tortoises of the kind which, as the Bible student is quick to recall, were such a familiar feature "among the creeping things" of the district around the Red Sea in the days of the exodus that the Mosaic law felt it necessary to brand them as "unclean" and to warn the tribes of Israel against eating them. [1]

The Aeginetan staters (which are much sought after by collectors) have another special distinction in addition to that of being the first known Greek money: they were the first coins to bear a design on both sides. On the reverse is a large square divided into four or five compartments—some of them wedge-shaped like windmill sails, others almost rectangular. This subdivided square was not there for decorative purposes; it had a definite use, for it helped to keep the flan (the lump of metal from which the coin was made) from turning and twisting on the die when hammered by the moneyer.

On these staters of Aegina, as on all other coins made within the next few centuries, the obverse and reverse faces are likely to appear in varying axial relationships to each other—sometimes top-to-top, sometimes topsy-turvy. This

[1] Leviticus 11:29.

is because the moneyer's pair of dies for the two sides were not fastened together in any fixed position. Such eccentricities furnish one clue to the fascination which ancient coins exert: the collector knows that machines played no part in their making, but that each coin is the result of painstaking individual effort on the part of some long-ago craftsman who, except for the dies, probably had no special equipment for his task. What he used were the ordinary tools of the smithy; hence it is not surprising that different specimens of the same coin often vary markedly in appearance, for the dies by which they were stamped frequently continued to be used long after they had been defaced by repeated battering with a heavy hammer against an anvil.

Yet despite this tendency to keep on using the same designs and the same damaged dies year after year without alteration, the geographic variety of coins was vastly greater in the world of two thousand-odd years ago than it is today; for every independent city, every tiny state or nation, had its own coinage, ornamented by local smiths or moneyers with designs of local significance, such as the crab of Akragas, shown here, which was an adroit advertisement of that city's most characteristic product. Scattered over the Mediterranean, other Greek colonies and city-states also produced their own money, stamped with their own representative designs, of which the barley of Metapontum and the cow of Dyrrhachium are typical.

During this period lettered inscriptions began to appear on coinage in addition to pictorial designs. Thus the silver stater of Thebes bears the abbreviated name of the magistrate who was responsible for producing it, and the didrachm of Akragas and tetradrachm of Athens display the names of the cities they represent.

The Athenian piece deserves particular mention because it is the first example to be shown in these pages of the coin which for centuries served as the international monetary standard of the Mediterranean world: the silver tetradrachm. The Athenians arrived at their monetary system by taking a Babylonian silver mina (a unit of weight very close to the modern pound) and dividing it into seventy parts which they made into coins called *drachmas*—also commonly referred to in ancient literature as *drachms* or *drams*. (The word *drachma,* incidentally, means "handful." It was given its additional numismatic meaning because the coin so named was equal in value to a handful of the little rods of iron or copper which commonly were used as small change.)

The drachma, worth perhaps eighteen cents in our coinage, was everywhere accepted as the small unit of value, while the tetradrachm, worth four drachmas, served a role very similar to that of our dollar for purposes of trade not only within Greece but in all the many lands which later came within the orbit of Alexander the Great and his successors. The establishing of so nearly uniform a currency over so wide a range was one of the truly outstanding achievements of the Greeks.

It may seem curious that the tetradrachm of Athens is so near in size to the didrachm of Akragas, worth only half as much. Similar inconsistencies in size will be noticed in later illustrations in this book. The fact is that it is quite impossible to judge the denomination of an ancient coin from its size. One reason for this variability in dimensions is that many cities and states, when they decided to issue money of their own, merely restruck with their own insignia the coins which came to them in the course of trade. Inevitably some of these coins had lost a little in size through wear and tear, and in the process of restriking they usually lost a little more, but the local magistrates apparently did not worry about this, being content to continue to call a tetradrachm a tetradrachm even after it had shrunk, for various reasons, to didrachm size.

With the growing multiplicity of coins, banks began to appear; but the average man distrusted banks, preferring to hide his savings in the ground or in odd corners of his house or wall. This is a habit for which we modern collectors can be deeply grateful, for often such hoards were not uncovered until centuries or even millenniums later. Particularly in times of extreme danger coins were likely to be buried. Such a time came between 500 and 449 B.C., during the Greco-Persian wars. It was about 500 B.C. that the Greek city-states along the coast of Asia revolted against the iron rule of Darius the Great, whose Persian Empire then included all of western Asia and Egypt. In this revolt, persisting for five or six years, the rebellious Greeks received some help from Athens; and when in the long run the insurrection was unsuccessful Darius decided to inflict punishment on Athens by extending his empire to Europe and by conquering Greece itself. There followed one of the most famous invasions in all history, and one of the most famous battles: that of Marathon in 490 B.C.

And here, in the beautiful Athenian tetradrachm portraying on its obverse the goddess Athena and on its reverse the big-eyed little owl which was Athena's symbol, we have a vivid reminder of the battle of Marathon—a piece of money which possibly may have been coined for the very purpose of commemorating that battle. (In the photograph of this tetradrachm it should be noted that by now the moneyers had advanced far beyond the plain incuse which the Lydians had known. Not only had the incuse evolved into something highly decorative; it had expanded to the very edge of the coin.)

The images of Athena and the owl alone would not be enough, of course, to associate this coin with Marathon, nor would the branch of Athena's sacred olive tree which appears at the far left on the reverse, just above the tip of the owl's wing. These were standard equipment of Athenian coins, for, as practically everyone knows, the ancient city of culture was named for the goddess of wisdom in return for her miraculous (according to the legends) gift of the olive trees which became the Athenians' chief source of wealth. No, the feature which makes us certain that this tetradrachm cannot have been coined until after Marathon is hardly visible except through a magnifying glass: a very tiny waning moon which the sharp-eyed may observe in the field between the olive and the owl.

And why a waning moon? Because the moon was on the wane on that fear-ridden occasion in 490 B.C. when the long-dreaded word reached Athens that the vast Persian army, made up of many times the number of men that Athens could possibly put under arms, was landing on the Plain of Marathon some twenty-odd miles northeast of the city. The Athenians, feeling themselves doomed, in desperation sent a swift messenger 150 miles down the Peloponnesian Peninsula to Sparta (he covered the distance in two days), imploring the Spartans to come to their aid without delay. Sparta at that time was not yet the bitter rival of Athens that it later became, but none the less the Spartans replied that their religion forbade them to march when the moon was on the wane; they were willing to help Athens, they said, but not now—not until the moon was full.

The Athenians, suspecting that the Persians would not be willing to postpone their plans of conquest to fit the phases of the moon, thereupon tackled the enemy without Spartan help. Outnumbered though they were, they emerged victorious through the brilliant strategy of their commander, putting the invaders so thoroughly to route that Darius was forced—for the time being, at least—to abandon his ambitious schemes.

From then on the waning moon was always, to the Athenians, a sign of good fortune. Along with the patron goddess Athena and her precious owl and olive branch it was memorialized upon their famous city's coinage, where it may be seen to this day.

After the victory at Marathon another swift runner sped to Athens to bear the news of victory. In honor of that feat long-distance races—particularly those in the quadrennial Olympic Games—have been known as marathon races. The Olympics (or, more precisely, the Olympian Games) were to the far-scattered Greeks as much a unifying force as were their Homeric legends and their common fealty to the gods and goddesses of Mount Olympus. The site of the Olympian Games was always the plain of Olympia in Elis, situated on the Peloponnesian Peninsula.

The coins of Elis were the ancient equivalent of modern "souvenir" pieces. Elis had no commerce or industry worth mentioning; practically its only industry was its tourist trade, brought by its quadrennial athletic contests and by its role as a year-round training ground for athletes. Tourists then, as now, brought plenty of money with them, and the Eleans found that the most profitable way of dealing with this influx of specie from all over the Mediterranean world was to melt it down and fashion it into new pieces of outstanding artistic appeal. In this way they achieved a remarkably wide circulation for their coins. That tourists from practically everywhere took these coins home as souvenirs of their visits to the great games is evident from the many places in which they have been found.

The drachm or drachma of Elis reproduced here originally bore on its obverse the laurel-crowned head of Zeus, the father of the gods, in whose honor the Olympian Games were held. (Similar crowns of laurel were placed upon victorious athletes' heads.) Alas for poor Zeus, however—this drachm, instead of being flat, was made slightly cup-shaped,

so that in the many centuries which have passed since it
was made its convex side has been almost obliterated.

Meanwhile the drachm's reverse, protected by its con-
cavity, shows hardly any wear; and after all these centuries
it remains almost as clear to our vision as it did to that of
Elean sporting fans and tourists. The design which it bears
is that of an eagle—a bird which, down through the ages,
probably has appeared on coins at least as frequently as
any other symbol. The Eleans, in their devotion to ath-
letics, probably viewed the eagle as representative of the
athlete's power, strength, and swiftness, and of the exalta-
tion which was the victor's reward. Coined twenty-three
hundred years ago, not long after the time when Malachi
was writing his final warning to the Jews, this Elean eagle
should by right be weak with advanced age, and almost
undecipherable; yet to our charmed eyes and probing
fingers it seems as ageless and powerful as if it had but
yesterday soared the skies and served as a medium of exchange in the marts of commerce in whatever parts of the
Mediterranean world Greek athletes visited upon returning
from their tests of strength and skill at Elis.

Even more appealing than the Elean drachm to the collector's aesthetic sense is the tridrachm of Corinth which,
bearing on its obverse a helmeted head of Athena, has upon
its reverse a figure of the fabled winged horse Pegasus so
very lifelike and convincing as to give us the feeling that
if Pegasus did not actually exist outside Greek mythology
he certainly should have done so! On this three-drachm
coin (of about the value of our half-dollar) Pegasus is glori-
ously free, still unfettered by the golden bridle whereby,
with Athena's help, the young Bellerophon eventually
caught and harnessed him. Produced somewhere between
400 and 338 B.C., this silver tridrachm, with its enchanting
Pegasus, was a day's wage for a worker living in Corinth

when that Peloponnesian city was famous for its beauty and wealth, and for the erotic practices which centered in the Temple of Aphrodite.

Gone, long gone, is that storied temple of vice; only a few crumbling pillars, renowned as the oldest Greek ruins extant, are left to remind us of ancient Corinth in its days of dubious glory. Yet this simple little coin which the Corinthians knew well—and which the Apostle Paul perhaps knew too, four hundred years later when he was living in Corinth—is still with us to marvel at and to cherish.

MACEDON: Silver stater of Philip II, 359–336 B.C., with the head of Zeus on the obverse and a naked horseman on the reverse. Philip's name is in the upper right field.

MACEDON: Gold stater of Philip II, 359–336 B.C. On the obverse is the head of Apollo, and on the reverse is a biga (two-horse chariot), with the name of Philip below.

MACEDON: Silver tetradrachm of Alexander the Great, 336–323 B.C. The obverse is filled with the head of Herakles wearing a lion's scalp; the reverse shows a seated Zeus holding an eagle and a scepter, with Alexander's name at the right.

MACEDON: Gold stater of Alexander the Great, 336–323 B.C., with the head of Athena in a Corinthian helmet on the obverse and a winged Nike on the reverse. Nike holds a wreath and a naval standard. Alexander's name is at the right.

39

ARADUS (now Arwad) in Phoenicia:
Silver stater, about 350–332 B.C. The
obverse bears the head of the Phoenician god Melkarth. The design on the
reverse represents a galley on ocean
waves.

ARADUS (now Arwad) in Phoenicia: Silver tetradrachm,
72–71 B.C., with the head of Tyche, patron goddess of Fortune. On the reverse is a wreath-encircled winged Nike.

MACEDON: Bronze coin of Cassander, about
306–297 B.C., with a head of Herakles in a lion's
scalp on the obverse. The reverse carries the inscription "King Cassander," with the figure of a
boy on a horse.

THRACE: Silver tetradrachm of Lysimachus, struck between 306 and 281 B.C. An idealized head of Alexander the
Great wearing horns of Ammon appears on the obverse; on
the reverse is the inscription "King Lysimachus," with a
seated Athena holding a winged Nike.

40

THASOS: Silver tetradrachm, struck after 146 B.C., bearing the head of Dionysos, the wine god, on the obverse, and a figure of Herakles, holding a club and a lion skin, on the reverse.

EGYPT: Silver tetradrachm of Ptolemy I, struck at Paphos in Cyprus between 305 and 285 B.C. Ptolemy's diademed head appears on the obverse; his name flanks the eagle on the reverse.

SYRIA (SELEUCID KINGDOM): Silver tetradrachm of Seleucus I, struck at the mint of Persepolis about 300–280 B.C. The obverse shows the head of Seleucus wearing a helmet covered with a panther's skin and adorned with the ears and the horns of a bull. On the reverse is Winged Victory (Nike) placing a wreath on a trophy.

SYRIA (SELEUCID KINGDOM): Silver tetradrachm of Antiochus I, struck at Seleucia-on-the-Tigris about 280–274 B.C. Antiochus's head appears on the obverse and his name on the reverse, flanking a figure of a seated Apollo holding a bow and arrow.

41

EGYPT: Gold tetradrachm of Ptolemy II, struck between 270 and 246 B.C. The obverse (at left) shows Ptolemy II with Arsinoë II, his sister-wife; the reverse shows their parents, Ptolemy I and Berenice I, as gods.

SYRIA (SELEUCID KINGDOM): Silver tetradrachm of Antiochus II, struck between 261 and 246 B.C., shows the head of Antiochus on the obverse, and his name on the reverse, with a seated Apollo. The tiny horse grazing beneath Apollo's figure is an emblem of Alexandria Troas, where the coin was struck.

EGYPT: Bronze coin representing Ptolemy V's wife, Cleopatra I (shown here in guise of Egyptian goddess Isis), who ruled Egypt from 181 to 173 B.C., during the minority of her son Ptolemy VI. The eagle and the legend on the reverse are almost obliterated on this specimen.

5

Kings of Daniel's Prophecies

And now the curtain descends upon the 400-year night between the Old and the New Testaments—the period of which we have no Biblical record (except in the books commonly called "apocryphal") because the scholars who first assembled the sacred writings decided that at this point the age of the prophets had come to an end! Yet oddly enough the coins of this era bear a particularly close relationship to the Bible, for the monarchs who had them struck are mentioned many times—sometimes specifically and sometimes in a thin veil of parable—in the prophecies of Daniel.

Greek power was rising now toward its climax—and its fall. The Persian Empire's hour of glory was nearing its end, for Alexander the Great was on the way, as Daniel had foretold when he said: "Behold, there stood . . . a ram which had two horns. . . . I saw the ram pushing westward, and northward, and southward; . . . he did according to his will, and became great. . . . And . . . behold, an he goat came from the west, . . . and the goat had a notable horn between his eyes. [Alexander wore a ram's horn as a symbol of strength and power.] And he came . . . and smote the ram, and brake his two horns: and . . . cast him down to the ground, and stamped upon him. . . . The he goat waxed very great: and when he was strong, the great horn was broken; and . . . came up four notable ones toward the four winds of heaven." [1]

As Gabriel explained Daniel's vision: "The ram which thou sawest having two horns are the kings of Media and Persia. And the rough goat is the king of Grecia: and the great horn that is between his eyes is the first king. Now that being broken, whereas four stood up for it, four kingdoms shall stand up out of the nation, but not in his power." [2]

These four kingdoms, with their "four notable ones," are the four main divisions into which Alexander's vast but short-lived empire was broken up after his early death. Coins of these four lands (Macedon, Thrace, Egypt, and Syria) form for some enthusiasts the basis for an exciting "collection within a collection": tangible mementos of those heirs to the great Alexander whom Daniel had prophesied.

Alexander was preceded by his father, Philip II of Macedon. Macedon was only a small country on the central Balkan Peninsula, north of Thessaly and northwest of the Aegean Sea (adjoining what is now Yugoslavia), but for centuries after Philip's day it exerted an influence far out of keeping with its size, for from within its borders came the military leaders who founded and carried on the Greco-Macedonian Empire, which continued to be Macedonian in its leadership even after its break-up into many quarrelsome parts. Of particular importance to numismatists is the fact that these far-flung Macedonian conquests were responsible for establishing all over the eastern Mediterranean world a stabilized and uniform currency, based on the silver unit of Athens.

Philip obtained military rule over Greece in 338 B.C. His

[1] Daniel 8:3–8.
[2] *Ibid.*, 8:20–22.

silver stater, shown here, may have been struck at about that date, although possibly it may be somewhat older, for Philip had been king of Macedon for more than twenty years before he became monarch of all Greece. The coin bears on its obverse a likeness of Zeus, father of the gods, not of Philip himself, for not yet had the time come when mortal sovereigns dared to risk the wrath of the gods by placing their own portraits on their coins. Philip was a lover of horses, so on its reverse his stater has a high-stepping horse ridden by a nude jockey bearing in his right hand a palm branch, token of victory. Beneath the prancing steed is the symbol so frequently associated with Zeus: a thunderbolt.

Far more valuable than this silver coin was Philip's stater of gold, bearing on its obverse the laurel-decked head of Apollo and on its reverse a chariot drawn by two horses. This gold stater was made at Amphipolis—a place which held particular significance for Philip because his seizure of this wealthy city in 357 B.C. had marked the beginning of the series of conquests through which he achieved his eminence. Amphipolis was a natural site for the making of coins, for it controlled the gold mines of Thrace, and from it flowed the precious metal which enabled this first great Macedonian king (and, after him, Alexander) to feed and equip and train his victorious armies.

Precious metals were of little avail to Philip, however, in stemming the intrigues which surged around his throne; and when as the result of these intrigues he was assassinated in 336 B.C., at the height of his power, he left the field clear for the restless young son who had been worried for fear his father was going to overrun so many countries that there would be no more worlds left for him to conquer when he reached the throne.

That young son, as history knows, lost no time in multiplying and extending the domain he had inherited. So busy, indeed, was this "he-goat" Alexander (whom elsewhere Daniel had foreseen as a leopard)[3] in pursuit of more and yet more conquests, that it is hard to believe he can have given much personal attention to the coins which were put out during his "third world kingdom"—the "kingdom of brass" which Daniel had predicted in interpreting Nebuchadnezzar's dream of a "great image."[4] Nevertheless many new coins were struck during Alexander's reign, and of these two are pictured here: a silver tetradrachm and a golden stater.

The tetradrachm is adorned by the head of the hero of Greek mythology who seems particularly appropriate to Alexander: Herakles (whom the Romans called Hercules). And what is that peculiar headgear which Herakles is wearing? It is a souvenir reminiscent of one of his twelve fabulous "labors": the killing of the Nemean lion with his bare hands. Alexander is said to have had a particular fondness for that legend, which told how Herakles tore from the lion's body the invulnerable skin, which arrows and spears could not penetrate, and adapted it for his own superbly defensive headdress; when he wore it his head was almost literally in the lion's jaws, while its forelegs were knotted around his neck and the rest of its impregnable skin hung down his back.

On the reverse of this Alexander-Herakles coin Zeus is found again; this time he is seated upon his throne (and certainly it is not a very impressive-looking throne), holding in his right hand an eagle and in his left a scepter.

The other coin of Alexander reproduced here—the gold stater featuring on one side a helmeted head of Athena and on the other the draped figure of Nike, winged goddess of

[3] *Ibid.*, 7:6.
[4] *Ibid.*, 2:31, 39.

victory—has an interesting link with modern times and, indirectly, with the history of the Jews during that 400-year period about which the Bible is silent. According to Flavius Josephus, the great Jewish historian of the first century of the Christian era, Alexander in the course of his epic march of conquest approached Jerusalem about 333 B.C. Having heard of the havoc wrought everywhere by the young Macedonian king and his legions, the Jews naturally were terrified at the news of the Macedonian invader's imminent arrival. In this crisis Jaddua, the high priest, besought God for aid.

Following God's counsel, the priest had the city adorned in its best, with its gates opened wide; and when the conqueror came into view the people of Jerusalem, dressed in white, went out to welcome him. Pleased at this reception, Alexander bid his soldiers stay their arms. Then, at Jaddua's invitation, he entered the great temple, where he was shown the prophecies of Daniel in which the overthrow of the Persian Empire by a Greek prince was predicted. His spirits raised high by this forecast of the success of his audacious enterprise, the Macedonian king told the Jews he was their friend, granted them free exercise of their religion and laws, and proceeded southward on his victorious way, leaving them and their property completely unharmed. [5]

Far less fortunate or less well advised, the inhabitants of Sidon, lying in Phoenicia a little more than a hundred miles north of Jerusalem, had seen their city ruthlessly conquered and ravaged. So thoroughly, indeed, did the invaders establish their sway that the surviving Sidonians did not even know that Alexander and his army had taken pains to bury in Sidon several copper pots literally filled with gold coins before they moved on toward Jerusalem. The gold coins were Greek staters of two kinds: those of

[5] Flavius Josephus, *Works*, Bk. II, Chap. 8.

Philip and those of Alexander, and so numerous were they that they represented wealth untold.

The surviving Sidonians, however, were far too occupied with fleeing for their lives to have any idea that a vast treasure had been buried in their midst. One of the places to which they fled was Aradus (now Arwad), a rocky island and seaport a hundred miles north of their own captured city. In Aradus various earlier generations of Sidonians also had taken refuge from the successive waves of invaders who plagued their homeland, and by the time the fugitives from Alexander reached there the city was busy enough and important enough to have its own coins. One of these, a Phoenician silver stater made between 350 and 332 B.C., is shown here. Tiny and extremely irregular in shape, the coin has upon its obverse the laurel-crowned head of Melkarth, the Phoenicians' Baal or presiding deity, and on its reverse a galley tossing on the waves.

Also reproduced here, for the purpose of indicating how in many places, if not in Jerusalem, those pervasive Greeks succeeded in permeating even the religion of the territory they invaded, is another coin of Aradus issued two centuries later. It is a silver tetradrachm of the first or second century B.C. On its face, in place of the Baal-worshipers' god Melkarth, is a veiled and turreted head of Tyche, Greek goddess of luck, while standing triumphantly on the reverse is Nike, Greek goddess of victory.

Ironically enough, however, by the time this latter coin came into circulation Nike was not doing nearly so well by the Greeks as she had in Alexander's time. And even that fabulous hero must have learned eventually that his best laid plans did not always work out as he intended, for it seems almost certain that when he ordered a fortune in Greek staters buried at Sidon he must have expected to reclaim it when he passed through that luckless city on his way back to Greece from Asia; but, as all history knows, Alexander never returned home. Defeated not by mortal enemies, but by his own over-indulgences, he died in Babylon in 323 B.C. Apparently the knowledge of the treasure he had buried in Sidon must have died with him, for not till nearly twenty-two centuries later (in A.D. 1850) were those copper pots filled with Philip's and Alexander's coins discovered. The major portion of this rich treasure trove from a long-gone epoch disappeared into the hands and pockets of the workmen who found it, but more than two thousand of the precious old Greek staters were salvaged by the governor of Sidon (now called Saida) to gladden coin collectors throughout the world.

"After his death," according to the Apocrypha, Alexander's servants "all put crowns upon themselves." [6] And certainly this exaggeration is not unduly extravagant, for the battling, jugglery, and confusion among Alexander's generals over the division of his empire continued actively for almost a quarter of a century after the leader's passing, and, even in the slightly more peaceful years which followed, the issue was never entirely settled. By the beginning of the third century B.C., however, the "four notable ones" prophesied by Daniel had more or less settled into their coveted places. They were Cassander of Macedon, Lysimachus of Thrace, Ptolemy of Egypt, and Seleucus of Syria.

Cassander was the son of Antipater, the trusted friend whom Alexander had left in charge of affairs at home when he set out upon his eleven-year tour of conquest in the East. His regency was challenged by Olympias, Alexander's mother, who tried to oust him from his post; but Antipater managed to remain in command, and succeeded to the leadership of Macedon upon Alexander's death. When Antipater died in battle, Cassander felt that he was

[6] I Maccabees 1:9.

entitled to succeed him; but Olympias opposed him, as she had his father; in fact, she was even responsible for having his brother and a number of his friends murdered. Not to be outdone, Cassander, a decidedly violent young man, promptly retaliated by attacking Olympias, crushing her army and killing her. Having disposed of Alexander's mother, he now felt safely entrenched as regent for Alexander's young son, Alexander IV; but for an individual of Cassander's driving ambition a mere regency was not enough: he had to be king or nothing. Therefore he finished paying off his grudge to his late monarch's mother by putting to death his ward, young Alexander IV, and the boy's mother, Roxana, widow of Alexander the Great.

Sole ruler now, he made his claim to Macedon's monarchy more secure by marrying Thessalonica, Alexander's half-sister, in whose honor he renamed the city of Therma, which continues to this day to be known as Thessalonica (or, more frequently, in its abbreviated form, as Salonica). As further steps to absolute power he waged war against various rivals for the throne until he emerged at last as undisputed king of Greece and Macedon.

Perhaps it is only natural that a ruler whose career was devoted so overwhelmingly to murder and intrigue should not have left any really handsome coins as mementos of his reign. Throughout the years of his regency Cassander continued Alexander's coins, and even after he became king he never put out any gold or silver pieces in his own name— which seems somewhat surprising, in view of his passion for personal aggrandizement. Even the four bronzes which he had struck were marked by nothing original; the one shown here (like two of the others) featured Herakles in his lion-skin headgear, just as Alexander's silver tetradrachm had done.

If Cassander's bloody reign brought no innovations in

the world of coinage, that of Lysimachus, one of Alexander's generals who took over the administration of Thrace upon his leader's death, has a very different story to tell. Up to the time of Lysimachus, it will be recalled, no piece of Greek coinage had ever borne the likeness of a mortal ruler. Lysimachus, however, was bold enough to break away from this tradition by issuing both gold staters and silver tetradrachms bearing the portrait of his illustrious predecessor, Alexander. Perhaps one reason why he dared to risk the displeasure of the gods in this way was that Alexander, in his later years of glory in the East, had reached the point of claiming godly lineage for himself, insisting that his mother had told him his real father was not Philip, but Ammon, the Egyptian Zeus.

Whatever the reason for them may have been, these staters and tetradrachms of Lysimachus were an outstanding innovation, being the first Greek coins to bear a regal image. They are, moreover, truly handsome pieces. A heroic head of Alexander wearing his ram's horn fills practically the entire field on the obverse, while on the reverse appears the seated figure of the goddess of wisdom, Athena, holding on her outstretched right hand the tiny winged likeness of Nike, goddess of victory. The pairing of Athena with Nike is an obvious attempt to portray Alexander's two ruling passions: the pursuit of learning and the pursuit of victory at arms; and the fact that Athena is helmeted and has a large shield leaning against her chair seems to tilt the scales a little (as Alexander himself eventually allowed them to be tilted) in favor of military might as opposed to wisdom.

It was in this same land of Thrace that, about a century and a half after Lysimachus, a silver tetradrachm was struck which brings vivid memories of the recurring conflicts between Greeks and Jews on the subject of religion.

This coin, issued on the island of Thasos, features the ivy-crowned head of the god of wine, Dionysos, whom the Thracians delighted to worship in ribald alcoholic rites. To the many Jews then living in Thrace such bacchanalian worship—so unlike their own solemn concept of religion—was a shocking sight, and they took no pains to conceal their disgust. Incensed at this "holier-than-thou" attitude, the worshipers of the wine god seized and branded great numbers of Jews at Thasos and throughout southern Thrace. And what was the brand they burned upon these luckless Hebrews? It was the bacchanalian symbol, so clearly preserved upon this Thracian tetradrachm: the ivy leaf!

Though Lysimachus of Thrace was the first to issue coinage commemorating a mortal king, he never advanced to the point of honoring himself on his coins. (Possibly this was because he was killed in battle before he had a chance.) No such modesty, however, restrained Ptolemy, the captain of Alexander's bodyguard who became the ruler of Egypt, where he founded a dynasty which lasted far longer than those of any of Alexander's other heirs. (The Ptolemies, incidentally, were just one step in the long succession of non-Egyptian "strangers" who have ruled Egypt since Ezekiel prophesied in 572 B.C. that because Egypt's sins had been so grievous "there shall be no more a prince of the land of Egypt.") [7] It is true that Ptolemy's earliest coinage as ruler of Egypt was in the conventional tradition, but soon this obedience to tradition ceased. When his kingship was assured by Cassander's murder of Alexander's young son Ptolemy took the notable step (probably about 310 B.C.) of placing his own portrait on his silver stater, thus producing a coin which has the distinction of being the first in history to show the head of a living ruler.

[7] Ezekiel 30:12, 13.

It is not surprising that some of the coins which Ptolemy issued as regent (before he became king in his own right) bear the likeness of Athena, for he, of all Alexander's successors, showed the greatest respect for wisdom. After a few military defeats—apparently realizing something of the futility of war—he turned his attention to reaching out not for territory, but for knowledge, seeking to encourage learning through such enduring contributions as the great library at Alexandria, which he founded.

His contemporary, Seleucus I of Syria, however, found the pursuit of knowledge of much less interest than the pursuit of land and power, and so successful was he in his ambitions that in time he became ruler of by far the major portion of Alexander's dominions, although his original share in the partition of the empire had been limited to Babylonia. In the early part of his reign Seleucus, like Ptolemy, paid the traditional obeisance to the gods in the design of his coins; the one shown here bears the head of Herakles in his lion's-skin headdress, with the reverse portraying a throned Zeus, plus the victory-symbol Nike. As Syria's ruler grew in confidence and power, however (and perhaps as he beheld enviously the Egyptian pieces which Ptolemy had put out), he too made use of coinage as a way of immortalizing his own likeness.

Like Alexander, Seleucus enjoyed wearing a horn as a symbol of his strength, and at least one of his coins pictures him with this formidable decoration. Nor did he restrict the use of horns to himself alone; his coinage also includes a number of horned elephants (apparently he had a particular fondness for elephants) and even a horse wearing a horn.

From the Bible student's viewpoint Seleucus' chief claim to fame lies not so much in his vast territorial conquests as in the fact that he built, about 300 B.C., the splendid city of Antioch (named in memory of Antiochus, his father) which later became such an important center for the early Christian missionaries. The name of Antiochus was commemorated also in the reign of Seleucus' son, Antiochus I, who succeeded his father on the throne, ruling from 280 to 261 B.C. The coins of Antiochus I, like those of many other monarchs of this era, represent a compromise between the desire for self-perpetuation and the desire for appeasement of the gods. In the silver tetradrachm shown here, for example, Antiochus I's head occupies the obverse, while on the reverse sits the god Apollo, armed with arrow and bow.

Although Ptolemy I and Seleucus I are the last of the four heirs of Alexander's power envisioned in Daniel 8:8, some of their troubled descendants in the Ptolemaic and Seleucid dynasties are prophesied just as specifically in the eleventh chapter of Daniel, and now we of the twentieth century of the Christian era are able to hold and to ponder some of the coins which, in the images they bear, reflect the strangely tangled lives and loves of these monarchs, which followed all too accurately the paths of dissension forecast by Daniel.

The chief actors in this tragedy of confusion were Ptolemy II of Egypt (commonly called Philadelphus), his two wives, his daughter Berenice, and his son Ptolemy III, together with Antiochus II of Syria and Laodice, his wife. Antiochus II and Ptolemy II are of importance in Biblical history, for the former founded Laodicea in Asia Minor, one of the seven cities to whose churches the seven letters of Revelation are addressed; while the latter, following his father's example in the encouragement of learning, gathered around him seventy or more of the finest scholars of his day for the purpose of translating the Hebrew scriptures into Greek—a notable forerunner of the eventual spread of the Judeo-Christian religion to the Greeks.

In their family lives, however, both Philadelphus and Antiochus II followed strange patterns. The first wife of Philadelphus and the mother of his children was Arsinoë I, daughter of Lysimachus, the king of Thrace who had shared with Ptolemy I, Cassander, and Seleucus I in the division of Alexander's empire. Philadelphus' great love, however, was not for his wife, but for his sister, whose name was also Arsinoë. Wherefore, living as he did in an age which winked at incest, he banished his wife and married his sister, who thus became Queen Arsinoë II. To her the second Ptolemy is reputed to have remained devoted for the rest of his life, and in her honor he had coined the remarkable gold tetradrachm (276-246 B.C.) which displays side by side the majestic Grecian profiles of this sister-and-brother husband-and-wife pair, with the reverse showing similarly arranged profiles (bearing a striking resemblance to their own) of their royal parents, Ptolemy I and Berenice, his queen.

Meanwhile Antiochus II (whose patrician profile appears on the silver Syrian tetradrachm shown here) had as his wife Laodice, in whose honor the city of Laodicea had been named. She had borne the king two children, but the time came when Egypt and Syria, warring as ever for power and preeminence, seemed to need a new dynastic alliance to bring peace between them. Therefore Queen Laodice was set aside, together with her two children, and in her place as Queen of Syria and wife of Antiochus II was installed young Berenice, the daughter of Ptolemy II by Arsinoë I, his banished first wife!

As if this weird succession of cruel events were not sufficiently tragic, the worst was yet to come. When Ptolemy II died in 246 B.C., his Syrian son-in-law promptly recalled Laodice and her children from exile, presumably planning to live comfortably with both his wives; but Laodice hastened to spoil this plan. Embittered by the outrageous treatment she had suffered, she poisoned her husband, Antiochus II, and caused the assassination of her rival, Berenice, together with the latter's infant son. As an epilogue to this series of tragedies Berenice's brother, who had succeeded to the throne of Egypt as Ptolemy III, avenged his sister's murder by waging war anew against Syria. He was successful in capturing Babylon and Susa, but then he was recalled home by a revolt in Egypt and became so engrossed in the affairs of his own kingdom that he allowed his Syrian holdings to slip out of his power.

This whole gruesome tale, as Bible students will recall, is forecast by Daniel's prophecy that "the king's daughter of the south shall come to the king of the north to make an agreement . . . but she shall be given up . . ." and so forth, right on down to the vengeance achieved by her brother. [8]

Through all the decades which followed, Syria and Egypt continued to quarrel and to effect uneasy temporary truces by way of interdynastic marriages, as in the case of Ptolemy V, who became king of Egypt when he was a small boy of seven or eight. In those early years of his reign, long before he came of age, his kingdom was attacked by Antiochus III of Syria, who seized Palestine, which throughout history has been the pawn of so many empire-builders. This fifth Ptolemy's reign is best remembered, perhaps, because it produced the Rosetta stone which, unearthed some twenty centuries later, has served as the vital key to the deciphering of ancient Egyptian manuscripts. The Rosetta stone was a memorial to Ptolemy V and to his wife, Cleopatra I, daughter of the very Antiochus III of Syria who had robbed his future son-in-law of part of his kingdom. Another memento of Cleopatra I is the curl-adorned coin,

[8] Daniel 11:6–7.

shown here, which was struck during her regency after her husband's death.

It is the nephew of this first Queen Cleopatra of Egypt, Antiochus IV of Syria (better known to history as Antiochus Epiphanes), whose hideous abuses of power bring us back to the central scene of Biblical narrative: Jerusalem. What gives him his page in history—a most infamous page—is the record of what he did to the Jews.

SYRIA (SELEUCID KINGDOM): Silver tetradrachm of Antiochus IV (Epiphanes), 175–164 B.C. The head of Antiochus is on the obverse; and on the reverse, surrounding a seated figure of Zeus holding Nike, is the inscription "King Antiochus, the god made manifest. Bringer of victory."

SYRIA (SELEUCID KINGDOM): Silver tetradrachm of Antiochus VII (Sidetes), struck at Tyre, 138–129 B.C. Antiochus's head is on the obverse; on the reverse is a standing eagle, with a monogram of Tyre surmounting the club at the left.

JUDEA: Silver shekel formerly believed to have been made about 139–138 B.C., at the time of Simon Maccabee, but now generally credited to the period of the First Revolt against Rome, A.D. 66–70. On the obverse is a chalice or pot of manna; the inscription is "Shekel Israel." On the reverse is a blossoming rod; the inscription reads "Jerusalem the Holy."

JUDEA: Bronze coin of uncertain denomination (perhaps 1/6 shekel), issued 141–135 B.C., during the high priesthood of Simon Maccabee. On the obverse are a lulab and citrons. On the reverse is a jeweled chalice or pot of manna; the inscription is "The redemption of Zion."

JUDEA: Bronze lepton ("mite") of John Hyrcanus, 135–104 B.C. On the obverse is a laurel wreath containing the inscription "John the high priest and the community of Jews." On the reverse are two cornucopias with a poppy head between them.

JUDEA: Bronze lepton of Judas Aristobulus, 104–103 B.C., inscribed on the obverse (within the wreath) "Judas the high priest and the commonwealth." On the reverse is a double cornucopia with a poppy head between its horns.

6

Pre-Roman Times in Palestine

Through all these years the Jews of Palestine, having been continually subject to foreign rulers, had had no coinage of their own. As their medium of exchange they used the drachms, tetradrachms, and other monetary pieces of Egypt, Syria, and the various Phoenician ports—pieces which bore images either of human rulers or of what the Jews considered heathen gods. Although the handling of such "idolatrous images" was contrary to the stern admonitions of their religion, circumstances forced them to forget their scruples. In this disregard of religious precept the priests of the temple may have had to play a leading part, for according to some authorities it was the temple's responsibility to establish the rate of exchange on the many different foreign coinages which flowed through Jerusalem's busy crossroads of trade.

Because Palestine's overlords—first the Persians, then the Greeks, and then the Ptolemies of Egypt—were generally fair and indulgent, the Jews of this period apparently had no particular desire either for their own coinage or for independence. Under the Ptolemies their lives were peaceful and prosperous. They had to pay tribute to Egypt, to be sure, but within Judea they enjoyed a large measure of freedom, and they and their religion spread widely and without opposition throughout the lands where Egypt ruled.

Many Jews had adopted the Greek language and customs

and were well on their way toward being assimilated into the Hellenistic world when Antiochus Epiphanes came along. Thanks to him, the trend toward assimilation came to a sharp halt, and the Hebrews entered on a brief but glorious period of independence or near independence which brought in its train the first coins Israel ever made.

This does not mean, of course, that Antiochus IV gave the Jews their freedom. Far from it! What he gave them was oppression so savage that for the time being it served to weld all the dissident factions of Israel in a passionate resistance to persecution, a common strength of desperation which enabled Judea to throw off the foreign yoke and, for a brief span, to achieve independence at last.

Antiochus Epiphanes was one of the sons of the Antiochus III who in 198 B.C. had captured Jerusalem from the boy king Ptolemy V and made Judea part of the Seleucids' Syrian empire. At first the Jews had thought that this turn of events was going to be fortunate for them; they optimistically believed that the rule of Syria would be an improvement over that of Egypt, for Antiochus III carried on the easygoing policy of Alexander and the Ptolemies by allowing the inhabitants of Palestine comparative independence and granting them complete religious liberty.

Their happiness under Syrian rule was short-lived, however. On the death of Antiochus III, in 187 B.C., his throne passed for twelve years to his son Seleucus IV, who, feeling that he was entitled to the wealth which the constant flow of trade brought to Jerusalem, proceeded to grab some of this wealth by plundering the temple. Yet what he did was nothing compared to the atrocities committed by his brother and successor, Antiochus IV.

This young man (he was not more than thirty when he seized the throne upon his older brother's death) thought very highly of himself. The name by which he was commonly designated, Antiochus Epiphanes, is usually translated as "Antiochus the Illustrious"; but even more ironical than this appellation, in view of his record, is the legend with which he marked his coins (witness the silver tetradrachm shown here): "Antiochus Theos Epiphanes"—meaning "The God Made Manifest."

Very soon after his assumption of power in 175 B.C., the distinctly ungodlike Antiochus began his persecutions of the Jews, but it was not until several years later that his evil genius reached its fullest flowering. In an attempt to conquer Egypt he was ignominiously stopped by Rome, the new world power, and so, bankrupt and humiliated, he abandoned the idea of tackling a foe his own size and vented his ire upon the Jews.

Taking Jerusalem by storm in 170 B.C., he plunged into an almost unbelievable orgy of cruelty. Not content with replenishing his treasury by levying huge taxes and by wholesale plundering and looting, he burned the city, slew vast numbers of the inhabitants, sold many others into slavery, and then embarked on a determined effort to stamp out all traces of Judaism. In the hideous course of this effort he profaned the temple in Jerusalem and the synagogues in all the outlying towns and villages, dedicated these places of worship to Zeus, made Greek rituals compulsory on pain of death, burned the sacred writings whenever he found them, and used every conceivable type of torture to compel the Jews to give up their religion and their customs.

Some of the Jewish people who were close to assimilation into the surrounding Hellenic world allowed themselves at first to be swept along by these horrendous changes, but the majority were so shocked by the wholesale desecration that they rallied to the support of the puritanical group of "Chasidim" (meaning "the pious") who were resisting

Antiochus IV with superb courage and spirit. It was in this hour of Israel's great need that there came into ascendancy that truly remarkable family which is known to history as the Maccabees. Through their inspired leadership, and through the unifying power of the Syrian King's persecution, the many Jews who had been gradually drifting away from the faith of their fathers were brought back into the fold, and Judaism acquired new strength.

No one with any knowledge of Jewish history needs to be reminded of the achievements of the Maccabees: how Mattathias of the Hasmonaean family, a priest at Modin, defied the Syrian oppressors, refused to sacrifice to a Greek god, and fled to the mountains with his five sons and others of the faithful to uphold the cause of liberty; how his son Judas, after Mattathias' death, displayed such astounding skill in war that people took to calling him Judas Maccabeus, or "The Hammerer"; how Judas defeated the Syrian generals and recovered the temple for Hebrew worship; how on Judas's death in battle his youngest brother Jonathan carried on his good work, building the Jewish religion to its former high standing; and how his older brother Simon, assuming the leadership of his people when Jonathan died, finally drove all Syrians from the citadel, won the independence of the Jewish nation, and gained for Judea the active support of Rome.

It was while Simon Maccabee was civil governor and high priest that the Jews reached an important milestone in their long history: the coining, for the first time, of their own money. Just thirty years after Antiochus Epiphanes had brought Judea to the verge of desolation and despair, another Syrian sovereign named Antiochus (Antiochus VII, surnamed Sidetes) wrote a letter to Simon Maccabee saying (among other things), "I give thee leave to coin money for thy country with thine own stamp." [1]

[1] I Maccabees 15:6.

Why it should have been necessary for Simon to receive this permission from the Syrian ruler is not quite clear, since history tells us that Judea already had achieved its independence. In any event the letter from Antiochus VII was followed in short order (139 B.C.) by the appearance of the very first coins the Jews ever made for their own use: some small coppers. There is striking contrast in design between these pioneer coins of the Jews and the coins of all the Greek-patterned world around them. Here are no kings and queens, no gods and goddesses. Instead, we see simple horticultural arrangements and inanimate objects, for the Israelites took seriously the second commandment's warning that "Thou shalt not make unto thee any graven image." [2] (Even in the coins of the new Israel, in the twentieth century after Christ, that commandment still is obeyed.)

Oddly enough they made no coins of silver, so far as is known. Probably this was because a number of neighboring cities, such as Aradus, Tyre, and Sidon, produced an abundance of silver coins (witness the tetradrachm of Antiochus VII shown here), and the Jews were content to use these and other foreign silver pieces which flowed into their country. Small coppers, on the other hand, were not likely to cross national borders in the course of trade, and for these lesser denominations of money there was, naturally, a large demand in a time and place when the great majority of the people were poor.

Yet despite this lack of Judean silver coinage it was generally believed until comparitively recent years that in the time of Simon Maccabee the Jews *did* coin silver shekels, and not a few numismatic publications of the past have attributed to the Maccabean epoch the silver shekel (illustrated) which later research has shown to belong to the period of the First Revolt two hundred years later.

Of bronzes or coppers, however, the independent Jewish

[2] Exodus 20:4.

nation produced an abundance. One of the largest of these is the piece shown here which was struck in the fourth year of Simon Maccabee's governorship. It is believed to have been worth one-sixth of a shekel, or about eleven or twelve cents in our coinage. The rather puzzling-looking objects on its obverse are a lulab and two citrons—the former being the bundle of palm and willow branches which the faithful, obeying the Lord's injunction to Moses, [3] carried in the right hand at the Feast of the Tabernacles, while bearing the citrons in the left hand. For the Maccabees the Feast of the Tabernacles held special significance because they well remembered that "not long afore" (during the cruel persecutions of Antiochus Epiphanes) "they had held the feast . . . when as they wandered in the mountains and dens like beasts." [4] On its reverse the coin features a jewel-rimmed pot of manna—presumably the one which Moses told Aaron to "lay up before the Lord." [5] Curving over the pot are the words "The redemption of Zion."

This sixth-of-a-shekel piece, small as it is, seems large by contrast when placed beside the tiny bronze or copper coin commonly called the lepton, which Judea apparently made in far greater quantities than any other kind of money. Nearly everyone who sees one of these minute lepta for the first time is moved to exclaim: "Ah, the widow's mite!"— and that, of course, is precisely what it is. To our ears *mite* may seem to be the more vivid term for this diminutive bit of metal, but in the Biblical era *lepton* was equally descriptive, coming as it does from the Greek word for "small" or "thin."

Since many of these mites were still in circulation a century and a half later, it is obvious that at the time of the

[3] Leviticus 23:40.
[4] II Maccabees 10:6.
[5] Exodus 16:33.

Maccabees there must have been an extremely large output of them. Even so, their total monetary worth probably was not very great, for they were valued at only 1/400 of a shekel or, in our terms, about a sixth of a cent. Because they were very tiny most of those which have been found in modern times are so corroded and worn down as to be mere slivers of metal; but if their designs and inscriptions are hard to decipher this condition is not entirely due to the inroads of time and wear. The trouble lies partly in the fact that lepta do not seem to have been as carefully made as larger coins. Perhaps they were too small for the moneyers' fingers to handle skillfully. At any rate it is evident that sometimes the flan was not properly placed on the die, with the result that the design on the coin's obverse was poorly centered. Just as often the crookedness of the mite's reverse shows that the punch was applied incorrectly to the flan. Frequently the mallet has been hammered too heavily on one side or too lightly on the other, producing an over-thin edge and an over-thick one.

In the light of modern time and labor values, however, the remarkable thing is not that these lepta were often made imperfectly, but that they were made at all, when we consider that each of them, though puny in size and in value, had to be stamped out individually by a trained artisan!

Both of the lepta shown here have on the obverse several lines of identifying inscription encircled by a wreath of laurel or olive, and on the reverse a poppy's head between two horns of plenty—symbols of the agrarian fruitfulness which was of such vital importance to a people haunted by racial memories of famine. Yet in spite of these surface similarities, the two lepta pictured represent widely varying phases of the Maccabees' rule, for the one on which the reverse design seems to have slipped halfway off the bottom was made during the beneficent leadership of John Hyrcanus, while the other is the product of the regrettable single-year's reign of John Hyrcanus's unworthy son, Judas Aristobulus.

John Hyrcanus, son of Simon Maccabeus, was high priest and governor of Judea for thirty years before his death in 104 B.C. He ruled vigorously, expanded his people's territory to include Samaria, Idumea, and lands east of the Jordan, and strengthened the Jews' friendly alliance with Rome—an alliance which he sorely needed to fend off the persistent encroachments of the Syrians, who again were causing trouble.

The source of the trouble this time was that same Antiochus Sidetes (Antiochus VII) who only a few years before had made so friendly a gesture toward the Maccabees as to give Simon permission to coin his own money. Now in 133 B.C. Sidetes seems to have suffered a change of heart, for he marched upon Jerusalem with the intention of destroying it. Some historians say that he actually *did* destroy it; but according to Flavius Josephus, the first century Jewish historian, John Hyrcanus was able to save his city by breaking open the 900-year-old sepulcher of David, wherein he found more than enough silver (three thousand talents worth nearly five million dollars) to persuade Antiochus VII to withdraw his troops. Bribery this may have been, but at least it was better, John Hyrcanus must have reasoned, than to allow the Holy City to suffer once again the fate it had undergone thirty-odd years before at the hands of Antiochus VII's infamous great-uncle, Antiochus Epiphanes.

On the whole the period of John Hyrcanus was a flourishing one for the Hebrew nation, but toward its close severe factional strife developed which forecast the end of Maccabean rule. This strife was between the Pharisees and the Sadducees, the two opposing Jewish parties whose differences in doctrine and policy were too involved and complicated to concern us here. Suffice it to say that the struggle between the two factions which cast a shadow over John Hyrcanus's later years eventually so weakened and disrupted Israel as to result, forty-one years after his death, in the end of Judea's independence.

Instrumental in starting his country on this downward path was John Hyrcanus's son, Judas Aristobulus, during whose short reign the second lepton shown here was coined. Unlike his father, grandfather, and great-uncles, this unscrupulous scion of a great family chose to assume the title of king, calling himself Aristobulus I; but he needed more than a royal title to make him—and his brother, sister-in-law, and nephews after him—worthy successors to the gallant Maccabees.

It was the nephews Hyrcanus II and Aristobulus II whose four-year civil warfare, reflecting the continued discord between Pharisees and Sadducees, brought to an unhappy ending the Maccabees' distinguished sway only a little more than a century after the priest Mattathias had taken to the mountains to plan the downfall of the tyrant Antiochus Epiphanes. Hyrcanus II and Aristobulus II were both determined to rule over Judea; and when, after years of fighting, they still were unable to settle their squabbles they went to Damascus to appeal for a verdict to Pompey, who was then at the height of his glory as commander of the Roman forces in Asia.

It was as if two mice had appealed to a cat to decide which of them was entitled to a piece of cheese. Pompey promised to come to Jerusalem to settle the matter, and when he came he *did* settle it to his own satisfaction. Like his more famous contemporary, Julius Caesar, he came, he saw, he conquered, with the result that in 63 B.C. Judea, after barely fourscore years of hard-won independence, passed under the rule of the new colossus, Rome. The Jews did not give in without a struggle, of course. In their desperate effort to keep Pompey's army from entering the temple at Jerusalem, twelve thousand lost their lives, but to no avail. Another province had been added to that fourth world kingdom which Daniel had prophesied. [6]

[6] Daniel 2:40.

SYRIA (SELEUCID KINGDOM): Silver tetradrachm of Philip II (Philadelphus), about 93–82 B.C., showing Philip's head on the obverse and a seated Zeus (holding Nike) on the reverse, with the inscription "King Philip, distinguished lover of his brother."

ROMAN REPUBLIC: Bronze as, about 196–173 B.C., showing Janus's head on the obverse. The ship's prow on the reverse is no longer recognizable.

ROMAN REPUBLIC: Silver denarius, about 124–103 B.C., with the head of Rome's patron goddess Roma on the obverse, and, on the reverse, a figure of Liberty, crowned by Victory, in a quadriga. An unusual feature of this coin is that the name of the magistrate M. Porc. Laeca appears partly on the reverse and partly on the obverse.

ROMAN REPUBLIC: Silver quinarius, about 90 B.C. The magistrate's name is featured prominently on the obverse to the left of the ivy-crowned head. On the reverse is seated Winged Victory, identified below as Victrix.

ROMAN REPUBLIC: Silver denarius, about 58 B.C., commemorating the conquest of Judea. The obverse shows King Aretas of Nabatea kneeling beside his camel, yielding to Rome. On the reverse Jupiter, driving a quadriga, is hurling a thunderbolt.

ROMAN REPUBLIC: Silver denarius, about 54 B.C., shows Cybele, mother of the gods, on the obverse, while the reverse portrays a bearded Jew kneeling beside his camel, yielding to Rome.

ROMAN REPUBLIC: Silver denarius, struck in Sicily about 42–36 B.C., showing on the obverse the head of Pompey, conqueror of Jerusalem, and, on the reverse, the figure of Neptune between the Catanian brothers carrying their parents on their shoulders.

PARTHIA: The obverse of a coin portraying King Orodes I, about 57–37 B.C.

JUDEA: Bronze lepton of Herod the Great, 37–4 B.C., bearing an anchor and Herod's name in Greek (abbreviated) on the obverse and, on the reverse, a double cornucopia with a caduceus between its horns.

ROMAN EMPIRE: Bronze coin (struck at Alexandria, Egypt) showing Livia, wife of Emperor Augustus. On the reverse, within an oak wreath, is the date: "L" standing for "year," "MA" for "41." Dating from the Battle of Actium, through which Augustus became emperor, this means A.D. 11.

ROMAN EMPIRE: Silver denarius of Augustus, struck in Caesaraugusta (Saragassa), Spain, about 25–22 B.C.

7

Rome Supreme

That Rome should have reached world leadership with such rapidity is one of the marvels of history. What had happened to the dominant Greeks, the powerful Seleucids, the imperial Ptolemies? Weakened by perpetual conflict, disunity, and abuse of power, these once-proud dynasties were no match for the buoyant, confident young nation which had sprung up only brief centuries before from the apparently insignificant Italic tribes along the plain of Latium and in the Palatine hills across the Tiber. In falling now under Rome's sway, Judea had almost innumerable companions.

Immediately before marching on Jerusalem, Pompey and his forces had just finished extinguishing the Seleucid dynasty in Syria. One of the last of the Seleucid kings was the Philip II whose likeness appears upon the silver Syrian tetradrachm shown here. This tetradrachm represents more than a mere coin of an obscure Syrian ruler. It represents the end of an era—the era of three centuries or more when the tetradrachm was the sole standard medium of exchange in the entire Mediterranean world. From now on, throughout the remainder of the Biblical period, the standard was to be a dual one: the tetradrachm had to share its sovereignty with the Roman denarius, while Latin, more often than Greek, was to be the language of the legends impressed upon coins.

The Romans' coinage, like so many other aspects of their civilization, was based partly on that of the Greeks; but it was also based upon the cumbersome system of money which they themselves had been using before they became a world power. Not until the fourth century B.C. had the emerging Roman Republic advanced far enough to begin issuing coins of its own. At first all of these pieces—huge, heavy things—were made of a crude sort of bronze: an alloy of copper, tin, and lead. Their weight was oppressive, for at this period the Romans had not yet grasped the idea of "token" coinage; they felt that the amount of metal in a coin must be approximately equal to its value.

Perhaps the first Roman money was the coarse, oblong piece of metal called an *as* which made its initial appearance about 348 B.C., bearing the crudely stamped figure of a cow, a sheep, or some other domestic animal. The word *as* in its original meaning was not the name of a coin, but the name of a measure of weight; it was the Roman pound, equivalent to a little under twelve of our ounces. And because the coin weighed as much as its namesake, it obviously was quite as unwieldy a thing to carry in any quantity as had been the shekels and talents of early Old Testament days.

Fifty years later the as still weighed a pound, but it had become almost round—a solid circle two and a half inches in diameter. Its guardian divinity, portrayed on the obverse, was the two-faced god Janus, keeper of the gate of heaven, who, with his unique ability to look in both directions at once, watched over all entrances to new places, times, and events (including the month beginning each new year, named in his honor).

Contemporary with the as were a number of smaller coins of the same type of bronze: the 2-inch *semis*, portraying Jupiter (the Roman Zeus); the 1¾-inch *triens,* picturing

Minerva (the Roman Athena); the 1⅜-inch *quadrans,* showing Hercules (the Roman Herakles); the 1¼-inch *sextans,*
featuring Mercury (the Roman Hermes); and the 1-inch
uncia, honoring sometimes Bellona, goddess of war, and
sometimes Roma, goddess of Rome. All of these coins bore
on their reverse the prow of a ship—representing, probably,
Rome's recognition of the importance of maritime supremacy in her conquest of the lands around the Mediterranean.

Less than a century after these heavy bronzes first
appeared, Roman traders found that their coins were of
little practical use abroad, for merchants in other countries
were accustomed to conducting business in silver, not in
bronze, which was far too bulky for convenient carrying.
Thus it was that between 280 and 265 B.C. the mint at
Rome began striking silver drachmas like the Attic ones.

Soon after these came into general use the huge as suffered its first reduction in size and in value, and the smaller
bronze pieces ceased to be made. By the close of the First
Punic War in 241 B.C., the as had shrunk from its original
impressive dimensions to two ounces; during the Second
Punic War (218-201 B.C.) it was cut to one ounce; and by
89 B.C. it had shriveled to a mere half-ounce. The Janus-
adorned as pictured here obviously must have been coined
after this gradual process of attrition was well on its way.

Meanwhile Rome had discarded its Attic-inspired silver
drachmas and had devised a new system of silver coinage
all its own. The principal piece, the denarius, was almost
the same as the drachma in weight and in value, being
worth about 15½ cents in our terms, or ten times as much
as the as. (In later years the value of the as was reduced to
one-sixteenth that of the denarius.) First issued about 180
B.C., it soon became the common medium of exchange, and
continued so into the days of the New Testament, when,
among other things, it was a day's wage for a laborer and

the money paid to the innkeeper by the Good Samaritan. [1]
To be sure, the New Testament always speaks of this coin
as a "penny" rather than as a "denarius." This is because
the scholars who produced the King James Version of the
Bible chose to translate it that way, being influenced, no
doubt, by the fact that Britain, which had used Roman
coinage during the island's centuries under Roman rule,
had continued—and in fact still continues—to represent in
writing the word "pence" by means of the symbol *d.*, which
originally stood for "denarii." Inasmuch as the denarius
had a far greater value than has the modern penny, this
unfortunately makes for confusion in interpreting some of
the New Testament's monetary references.

The denarius of the Republic had on its obverse the
head of the guardian goddess Roma wearing her winged
helmet. Sometimes back of her head and sometimes under
her chin (as in the coin pictured here) was the Roman
numeral X, signifying that this coin had a value ten times
that of the as. The earliest denarii displayed on their reverse
the Dioscuri—the twin gods Castor and Pollux—mounted
on horseback; but those coined somewhat later (like the
denarius illustrated here, which was made near the end of
the second century B.C.) presented a reverse bearing the
characteristic four-horse Roman chariot known as the
quadriga, driven by Jupiter.

Companion pieces to the denarius, though less common,
were the silver quinarius and sestertius, with values equal
to one-half and one-fourth that of the denarius, or about
eight cents and four cents, respectively. The small silver
sestertius soon ceased to be made, but an entirely different
piece of the same name—a large bronze—later became a
popular and decorative coin of the Roman Empire. Most of
these early Roman coins were rather crude and ugly com-

[1] Matthew 20:1, 2; Luke 10:35.

pared to the Hellenic ones; but as time went on they became
far more artistic and expert in workmanship.

Long before Pompey's conquest of Jerusalem in 63 B.C., the
denarius had come to be used and accepted over as wide an
area as the drachma and tetradrachm had been in the preceding centuries, and the idea of designing special issues to fit
special occasions already had become popular. It is not surprising, therefore, that within a few years after Judea was
added to the sprawling new world kingdom several denarii
were issued to celebrate Rome's acquisition of a new
province.

One of these, struck about 58 B.C. in honor of Marcus
Aemilius Scaurus, one of Pompey's chief aides, commemo-
rates the annexation of Judea by showing Aretas, king of
the Nabatean Arabs who had aided the Maccabean
Hyrcanus II in his conflict with his brother just before the
Romans' intervention. Aretas is kneeling beside his camel
and submissively proffering to Rome the laurel of victory.
On the reverse we again behold Jupiter in his quadriga.

Another denarius, issued three or four years later, commemorates the capture of Hyrcanus' brother and enemy,
Aristobulus II, by showing him on the reverse kneeling
humbly (also by a camel) to extend a symbolic palm to
Rome, the identity of the surrendering warrior being established by the inscription " Judaeus." At this period nearly
all Roman coins still paid more homage to the gods than
to human heroes, and this one, showing on its obverse the
turreted head of Cybele, mother of the gods, is no exception.
A third denarius of this period, however, makes it apparent
that a new trend toward human hero-worship by numismatic means was now emerging. This piece, one of the first
of Roman coinage to present the portrait of a mortal, shows
the great Pompey himself; on its reverse is a charmingly
animated, if somewhat impressionistic, version of the Roman

legend of the two Catanian brothers who, when Mount Etna made its first recorded eruption in 476 B.C., left all they possessed in order to carry their parents to safety.

Pompey, eager to return to Rome, and concerned with numerous other matters more important than the small province of Judea, was willing to allow the Maccabean king Hyrcanus II to remain as Judea's governor under Roman overlordship, and for a few years Hyrcanus was able to stay on in that capacity; but after Pompey's defeat at Caesar's hands even this vestige of Maccabean power disappeared, and the day of the Herods— so infamous in New Testament history—began.

The founder of this line was an Idumean named Antipater, who had gained his foothold in Palestine by giving refuge to Hyrcanus II during that luckless monarch's conflicts with his brother. Antipater cemented his power by giving valuable aid at Alexandria to Julius Caesar, who promptly rewarded him by granting him Roman citizenship and appointing him procurator of Judea. His ascendancy was brief, however, for he was assassinated, and his son Herod was appointed to succeed him.

It was at this point that one of the most bizarre episodes in all Palestine's troubled history occurred. One of the Maccabees, Antigonus, son of Aristobulus II, being determined to regain the power which had belonged to his family, succeeded in enlisting the aid of the Parthians, that almost fabulous race of nomadic horsemen and archers whose stronghold lay northeast of Palestine, between Arabia and the Caspian Sea. With these formidable allies Antigonus invaded Judea in 40 B.C., forcing Herod to flee to Rome for protection. For three years Antigonus and his Parthians maintained a shaky rule over the land. It was during this period that the odd-looking silver coin of Parthia shown here was put into circulation to add to the already tangled web of Judean currencies. But their reign came to an end in 37 B.C., when Herod returned to Jerusalem in a blaze of glory, backed by Rome's power and equipped with the impressive title of King of Judea, which Marc Antony had arranged for him to have.

That this first of the Herods was an adroit politician is indicated by the fact that in 31 B.C., when Antony, his patron, was overwhelmingly defeated at Actium by Julius Caesar's grandnephew Octavius, Herod promptly made his peace with the victor and remained throughout the rest of his life a great favorite of the man who was to become, as Augustus, the first and perhaps the greatest of Rome's emperors.

Herod's was a strange life, filled with contradictions. He tried his best to mollify the Jews by proclaiming himself a convert to Judaism, publicly observing the ancient Hebrew Law, starting to build a great temple, beautifying Jerusalem with many impressive buildings, and marrying Mariamne, granddaughter of two of the Maccabean kings. At the same time his private life was fantastically marred by luridly evil patches. His marriage to Mariamne, contracted to win the favor of the Jews, was but a fleeting incident in a long procession of at least ten matrimonial ventures; eventually he killed his Maccabean wife in a fit of jealousy, clinching this murder later by executing two of her sons. This was the Herod—somewhat incredibly called "Herod the Great"—who was ruling at the time of Jesus' birth and who ordered the massacre of the innocents of which Matthew tells so eloquently. [2]

This first of the Herods, like the others after him, coined bronze money (a battered specimen of which is reproduced here), but Judea's principal monetary standard continued to be the silver denarius coined in Rome. Lesser coins than

[2] Matthew 2.

the denarius were made in Rome too, of course, and one of
these was the dupondius, a good-sized bronze or brass piece
valued at about two cents in our money. A dupondius of
particular interest is the one pictured here, whereby the
emperor Augustus sought to perpetuate the memory of
Livia, his beautiful wife.

Whether Livia deserved this tribute is a matter which is
open to question, for whereas some historians are convinced
that she was a loving and dutiful wife there are others who
feel that she was responsible for the fact that the great Augustus had no direct heirs to succeed him upon his death.
The trouble was that Livia, though only eighteen at the
time of her marriage to the then Octavius in 38 B.C.,
already possessed two sons by an earlier husband whom
Octavius persuaded her to divorce in his favor; and when
no sons came to bless her marriage to Octavius-Augustus
she demonstrated a remarkable talent for pushing her older
son, Tiberius, into the line of direct succession, although
Augustus possessed some grandsons by a daughter of his
first marriage, as well as several promising nephews, who
would seem to have been more logical candidates.

One after another all of these kinsmen of Augustus perished, sometimes in rather mysterious circumstances, until
there was none left to inherit the imperial throne but
Livia's son Tiberius, whom she had persuaded her husband
to adopt. As the tragic roll of deaths among the emperor's
natural heirs mounted to its climax, public suspicion began
to center upon Livia. People whispered that what seemed
to be the hand of Fate was, in brutal fact, the hand of the
empress, operating not directly, of course, but by remote
control. Perhaps she was a woman unjustly accused;
perhaps the muffled charges against her were unfounded.
Certainly they never were proved; but at least they left a
lingering aroma of mystery which, all these many centuries

later, adds a certain piquancy to this Livia-adorned dupondius which, coined at the outset of the Christian era, is
still available for us to wonder at and admire.

Through the miracle of coinage, almost impervious as it is
to the ravages of time, we of the twentieth century are able
to study the features not only of the enigmatic Livia but
also of her illustrious husband, founder of the Roman
Empire, whose handsome head appears on a whole series
of silver denarii struck in the long years of his reign, from
27 B.C. to A.D. 14. To historians Augustus may be known as
the presiding genius of Rome's "Golden Age," but to Bible
students he must always be remembered primarily as the
Caesar Augustus from whom "there went out a decree . . .
that all the world should be taxed." [3]

That decree sent Joseph and Mary to Bethlehem for en-
rollment because Joseph "was of the house and lineage of
David" and Bethlehem was "the city of David." [4] That
decree caused Bethlehem to have its beautiful stories of the
shepherds, of the angels' song, and of the coming of the
Magi. That decree placed a shining star over Bethlehem
forever.

[3] Luke 2:1.
[4] *Ibid.*, 2:4.

CHIOS: Bronze assarion, about 84–44 B.C. On the obverse is the badge of Chios, a winged sphinx; on the reverse is an amphora, flanked by "Chios" (left) and a magistrate's name (right).

ROME: Bronze as of Augustus, struck in the East between 27 B.C. and A.D. 14.

TYRE: Silver tetradrachm or shekel, 106–105 B.C. The head of the god Melkarth appears on the obverse; on the reverse is an eagle standing on a rudder, with the inscription "Tyre the holy and inviolable."

JUDEA: Bronze lepton ("mite") of Alexander Jannaeus, 103–76 B.C. The obverse contains an anchor and the now illegible name of the king; an eight-spoked wheel appears on the reverse.

JUDEA: Bronze lepton of Herod Archelaus, 4 B.C.–A.D. 6. The obverse shows a bunch of grapes, with the name of Herod in Greek; the reverse has a helmet with cheek pieces, two crests (probably of horse's hair) on the left and on the right, and a small caduceus below.

JUDEA: Bronze lepton of Valerius Gratus, procurator under Tiberius, coined in A.D. 18–19. On the obverse, within an olive wreath, is abbreviated "Tiberius Caesar." On the reverse, in addition to a palm branch, are the date (fifth year of Tiberius's reign) and the name of Julia, second wife of the emperor.

JUDEA: Bronze lepton of Pontius Pilate, procurator under Tiberius, coined A.D. 30–31. On the obverse is an augur's wand encircled by the name (here largely illegible) of Tiberius. The date (seventeenth year of Tiberius's reign) appears within the wreath on the reverse.

ROME: Silver denarius ("tribute penny") of Tiberius,
A.D. 14–37. The inscription encircling the emperor's head
on the obverse reads, "Tiberius Caesar, son of the divine
Augustus." On the reverse is Livia, mother of Tiberius, in
the role of Pax, holding a branch and a scepter.

ANTIOCH (in Syria): Silver tetradrachm of Augustus,
A.D. 5. A portrait of the emperor is on the obverse; on the
reverse is the Tyche of Antioch, with the river Orontes at
her feet.

8

Coins That Jesus Knew

Many of us—even coin collectors—have been so in the habit of accepting as "gospel truth" Paul's statement that "the love of money is the root of all evil" [1] that we cannot help feeling a sense of shock, almost of sacrilege, in the suggestion that Jesus knew and used the coins of his day. Yet every Bible student is aware that Jesus not only had personal contact with money but also drew, in his teachings, a number of lessons from its use. Because currency was such an important part of daily human life, even this least mercenary of teachers could not possibly overlook its significance. In fact he chose as one of his disciples Matthew, whose vocation—the collecting of tolls and customs—had had to do strictly with the raising of money.

It is true that Jesus condemned private wealth and that he and his disciples depended for the filling of their simple needs largely upon the charity of the people they met. It is true too that he told his disciples, "Provide neither gold, nor silver, nor brass in your purses, nor scrip for your journey." [2] Yet we know that the disciples sometimes *did* have to use money, as in the first year of their master's ministry when he waited one day beside the well at Sychar, "for his disciples were gone away unto the city to buy meat." [3] And certainly if they had not been accustomed to purchasing

[1] I Timothy 6:10.
[2] Matthew 10:9–10.
[3] John 4:8.

food they would not have asked him on that day two years later "in a desert place," when there was a multitude of five thousand to be fed: "Shall we go and buy two hundred pennyworth of bread, and give them to eat? " ; [4] nor would there be that famous reference in John to Judas's possession of the money bag with which he might "Buy those things that we have need of against the feast." [5]

Because the accounts of Christ's life and teachings abound in such references as these to gold and silver and money, there is a natural desire on the part of the reader or hearer to know precisely what pieces of money were meant. In most cases, however, it is practically impossible to make an exact identification. Even where we do know the name of the specific coin in question there is still great difficulty if we try to evaluate it, for not only did most coins of this period bear no indication of their value, but the values of the various denominations changed greatly from time to time and the exact relation of copper or bronze or brass coins to silver ones is frequently a mystery.

Serving further to confound the confusion is the fact that coins from so many different sources were current in Palestine: coins of the Roman governors, coins of the Herodian vassal kings, coins from Rome's Asian mint at Antioch, coins sometimes from far-away Rome itself, Maccabean coins dating back to Jewish independence, and coins from innumerable other authorities and monetary systems, including above all a vast number from places where the Greek influence and language still were dominant. Rome had achieved political and military supremacy, but in a large part of the Mediterranean world the Greek names for money continued to be in general use—as was, in fact, the Greek money itself.

[4] Mark 6:37.
[5] John 13:29.

Despite the unquestionably sound scholarship of those who translated the New Testament into English, they seem to have done their share to add to the confusion about the money of Jesus' time. Not only were they responsible for the identification of "denarius" with "penny," already mentioned, but for some unexplained reason they chose to render two entirely different Greek words as "pieces of silver" in the English version, and to do the same thing with "farthing."

Yet it is just such uncertainty as this that makes coin collecting a challenging hobby. Even though it is not possible to say exactly how much the mites were worth which the poor widow gave to the temple treasury, or to evaluate beyond a doubt in terms of our money the thirty pieces of silver for which Judas betrayed Jesus, we at least have enough clues to set us on the trail.

Perhaps the puzzle of the "farthing" is as good a one as any to start with. In the gospel accounts this name for a coin is used four times [6]—the most familiar of these, probably, being the occasion when Jesus asked: "Are not two sparrows sold for a farthing?" Naturally most of us, on hearing this query for the first time, assume that the farthing was a coin of common currency in Palestine. Actually, the word here given as "farthing" was "assarion" in the original, leading us to believe that it may have been one of numerous Greek or Roman assaria which were circulated in Palestine in the period of Jesus and to which the British translators of the King James Version chose to give the name of a low-value contemporary British bronze coin with which they knew their readers would be familiar. (The assarion reproduced here is from Chios, the island in the Aegean Sea reputed to have been the birthplace of Homer.)

[6] Matthew 5:26; 10:29; Mark 12:42; Luke 12:6.

"Very good," we begin to think. "So the farthing was an assarion, probably Greek." But no, identification is not that simple, for other authorities contend that "farthing" was merely a free-handed translation for the familiar Roman as. Considerable substance is given to this belief by realization that in Luke's version of the sparrow-farthing query ("Are not five sparrows sold for two farthings?")[7] the word translated as "two farthings" was originally "dupondius," and a dupondius, of course, was worth twice as much as an as. If "farthing" *does* stand for "as," the coin may possibly have been one of the bronzes adorned with the head and laurel wreath of Caesar Augustus which were made during the first emperor's reign for use in Rome's Asiatic provinces. These Asiatic pieces were turned out by the mint at Antioch which Augustus had founded, and since communication was frequent between that city and the Holy Land the coins made there were widely used in Palestine.

But Jesus and his disciples probably would have been familiar with this particular as even if it never had come into trade in Palestine, for in the summer of the year 29, it will be remembered, they spent six days far up in the northeast, beyond the sources of the Jordan, in the vicinity of the town at the foot of Mount Hermon which the Greeks had called Paneas after their lusty god Pan, to whom they had also dedicated the great cave nearby which is the source of the Jordan's easternmost branch. Some years before Jesus' pilgrimage to this point (which was, incidentally, the farthest north he ever traveled), Philip the Tetrarch, one of the numerous sons of Herod the Great, had established his residence at Paneas and changed its name to Caesarea Philippi.[8] This Philip was the Herodian prince who later

[7] Luke 12:6.
[8] Now known as Baniyas in southwestern Syria.

had the dubious distinction of becoming the husband of
the dancer known to secular history as Salome. The coming
of Jesus to Caesarea Philippi occurred only a few months
after Salome (mentioned in the Bible only as "the daughter
of Herodias") had claimed the head of John the Baptist as
a reward for her dancing. [9]

Christ's visit to this region was a significant turning point
in his life, being marked, as it was, by his transfiguration
and by his decision to go to Jerusalem to almost certain
death. And, on a far more mundane plane, it was also one
of the times when he and his disciples most certainly must
have needed to make use of money, for in this strange land
dedicated to Pan they were a little band of total strangers—
nameless wanderers who probably would have had a hard
time filling their daily needs for food without the help of
the communal money bag which Judas carried. [10] While in
and around Caesarea Philippi they can hardly have
avoided some contact with the Augustan as, for in this
region it was one of the commonest of all coins—such a
coin as the disciples may well have used when going "into
the city to buy meat."

Thus it seems fairly sure that Jesus must have known
both the assarion and the Asiatic version of the Roman as,
but certainly he did not know them as "farthings." The
mystery becomes even more complex when we find various
authorities advancing still other claimants to the title of
"farthing": the dilepton, the quadrans, the chalcus, the
small bronzes of the Herods and of the Roman procurators—at one time or another all of these have been identified as farthings. In view of these doubts and contradictions,
perhaps it may be just as well to let the puzzling farthing
rest in peace and to move on to somewhat surer ground by

[9] Matthew 14:6–11; Mark 6:22–28.
[10] John 12:6; 13:29.

tackling the imagination-stirring incident of the coin in the fish's mouth which occurred, Matthew tells us, soon after Jesus' return to Galilee from Caesarea Philippi.

Everyone is familiar with this story: how "when they were come to Capernaum, they that received tribute money came to Peter, and said, Doth not your master pay tribute?" [11] The required tribute in this instance was not the tax exacted by the Roman overlords, but the fee levied upon all adult Jews from the time of Moses as "an offering unto the Lord." [12] Through the centuries this levy varied in amount; at the time of Jesus it was half a shekel (roughly thirty-two cents, or sixty-four cents for two persons). Being without "gold, nor silver, nor brass," Jesus and Peter had no such sum available, but Jesus, it will be recalled, told his disciple, "go thou to the sea, and cast an hook, and take up the fish that first cometh up; and when thou hast opened his mouth, thou shalt find a piece of money: that take, and give unto them for me and thee." [13]

What "piece of money" would that have been? (This is assuming, as we must, that the coin actually was found in the fish's mouth; Matthew tantalizingly stops his account short at that point and leaves our curiosity unsatisfied.) Some translators have given it as "shekel," and certainly the easiest assumption would be that the coin so providentially provided for a Hebrew levy should have been a Hebrew one, but unfortunately the evidence seems to indicate that at this period the Jews had not yet made any silver shekels of their own. Therefore the coin in the fish's mouth must have been some other silver piece of common usage which was accepted as of shekel value. Such a coin was, of course, the tetradrachm, which for so many years had served as the international standard of exchange.

[11] Matthew 17:24.
[12] Exodus 30:13, 15.
[13] Matthew 17:27.

But what kind of tetradrachm? There were tetradrachms from Syria, tetradrachms from Egypt, tetradrachms from any number of other places. The two likeliest candidates are those from Antioch and Tyre. Since Antioch was the capital of Rome's Asiatic provinces, and since its coins were widely used in Palestine for trade, its tetradrachm might at first seem to be the logical choice, but in point of fact this was not the case, for by Talmudic law the money of Antioch was excluded from the temple treasury, whereas coins made in Tyre were acceptable. [14]

The basis for this distinction apparently had nothing to do with the matter of "idolatrous" designs which sometimes caused the Jews to ban certain coins, for obviously the image of the Phoenician god Melkarth on the Tyrian tetradrachm was quite as "idolatrous" as the representations of the emperor Augustus and the Roman goddess Fortuna on Antioch's silver piece of equal value. No, the reason why the tetradrachms of Antioch were banned by the priests was that they did not contain enough silver to meet the Mosaic specifications for temple contributions. [15] Those of Tyre, on the other hand, were heavy enough to be satisfactory. This knowledge of rabbinical requirements makes us seem fairly safe in deciding that Tyre's tetradrachm (often referred to as a "shekel") must have been the coin which Peter presumably found in the fish's mouth.

A far more famous encounter with the business of temple money collecting than that incident at Capernaum was in the following spring when Jesus and his disciples went to Jerusalem for the Passover. The place was crowded both with Roman soldiers and with excited Jews from all parts of the known world who had made pilgrimages to the Holy City to celebrate the feast of Jewish independence. In the temple the confusion was tremendous, for all the pilgrims had to make cash offerings and yet by Hebrew law they

[14] James Hastings, *Dictionary of the Bible*, III, 422 and 432.
[15] Exodus 30:13.

could not use the coins which they had brought with them, but had to procure from the money-changers who cluttered the outer courts something which would be acceptable to the treasury.

These money-changers were able to set their own rates of exchange for the wide variety of coins offered them, and because many of them were highly unscrupulous men they waxed rich in purse at the expense of the devout. Naturally they were deeply resented, and when Jesus and his followers wrecked their tables and cast them out, accusing them of transforming "the house of prayer" into "a den of thieves," [16] there was wide popular approval; but the enmity of the priests had been incurred.

It was on the day following this display of righteous wrath that Jesus made it his business to sit close to the temple treasury and watch the people casting in their offerings, thus providing us with the observation about the widow's mite which has come down through the ages with undiminished force: how "many that were rich cast in much," but "a certain poor widow" who "threw in two mites . . . hath cast more in, than all. . . . For . . . they did cast in of their abundance; but she of her want did cast in all that she had." [17]

Because of the close association of the mite, or lepton, with the last days of Jesus' life, this tiny coin awakens in the collector an interest which is out of all proportion to its size. Nobody knows, of course, just which kind of lepton Jesus saw the widow give. It may have been any of a wide range of possibilities, for coins lasted far longer then than they do now; the ancients seldom carried them around in pockets and handbags to be rubbed together and defaced. Even the copper pieces coined by the Maccabees were still

[16] Matthew 21:13.
[17] Mark 12:41–44.

in circulation to some extent; in fact the lepton of Alexander Jannaeus of the Maccabean dynasty is believed to have been one of the favorite pieces for the temple offering, even though it was by now over a hundred years old.

This Maccabean lepton (pictured here) may have been one of the two which the widow gave, or she may have offered grape-and-helmet-adorned lepta of Herod Archelaus, the son of Herod the Great whose reign had inspired such fear in Joseph as to cause him to take Mary and the young child Jesus to Galilee instead of to Judea upon their return from Egypt.[18] Another possibility is a lepton of Valerius Gratus, the immediate predecessor of Pontius Pilate as governor of Judea, or—perhaps the most interesting candidate of all—one or more of the lepta of Pilate himself.

The lepton or mite of Pilate shown here is a particularly revealing one, for it pictures a device which played an active part in the life not only of this vacillating governor of Judea at its supremely important moment of history but also in that of his ruler and patron, the emperor Tiberius. This device is an augur's wand. The Romans felt that interpretation of the will of their gods was a matter for careful training; accordingly they provided a college of augury where selected pupils learned to determine the portents of such phenomena as lightning flashes, flights of birds, positions of clouds and stars, the rush of the winds, the whir of insects, and even a cat's crossing of one's path. Graduation from this college raised a man to a level far above his fellows. Before he became governor of Judea, Pilate was an augur, and quite possibly it may have been his eminence in this field which won him the emperor's favor, for Tiberius was an ardent believer in augury.

Pilate, as the agonizing events of those next few days of

[18] Matthew 2:22.

crisis were to show, was a vacillating man, a man of para-
doxes; and certainly one of the most paradoxical things
about him was the way in which, at the very time when he
was trying to get along comfortably with the Jews, he had
the effrontery to provide those devout people of Judea for
their daily use a coin bearing, in its augur's wand, a symbol
of one of the very customs which the Children of Israel had
been specifically taught to abominate. Ever since the days
of Moses they had been warned repeatedly against divining
or augury in any form. [19]

Quite as important to the Jews as their hatred of the
type of portent-interpreting which Pontius Pilate practiced
was their insistence that no mortal ruler—no Roman Caesar—should be worshiped as a god. Throughout their
domination by Augustus and his legions they had held out
stubbornly against the growing cult of emperor worship.
There could be no god, they insisted, but the one true God.
Yet now, with Augustus dead, they were forced by practical
necessity to make use of coins on which Tiberius, Augustus'
stepson and successor, was identified as "son of the deified
Augustus."

It was one of these coins of Tiberius, his silver denarius,
which the high priests Caiaphas and Annas used in their
attempt to rid themselves of the unwanted competition of
the intruding preacher from Galilee who in this April of
the year 30 was magnetically drawing great crowds to hear
his teachings. It would be a simple and easy thing, they
reasoned, to trap Jesus into criticism of the tribute tax im-
posed upon the Jews by Tiberius and then to see to it that
his critical words reached the ears of the emperor's repre-
sentatives in Palestine. Punishment of such heresy would
follow speedily, they felt sure, and then no longer need they
have cause to be jealous of this presumptuous Jesus of Naz-

[19] Deuteronomy 18:10–14.

areth who was going up and down the land teaching a new way of life.

So it was that they went to Jesus with their carefully set trap, asking, "Is it lawful to give tribute unto Caesar, or not?"

At Jesus' request, "Shew me the tribute money," they displayed a coin (almost without question a duplicate of the denarius of Tiberius which is pictured here) about which he asked, "Whose is this image and superscription?" To this they replied "Caesar's," and then were temporarily nonplused when he told them, "Render therefore unto Caesar the things which are Caesar's; and unto God the things that are God's." [20]

That the newcomer from Nazareth had skillfully avoided condemning the tribute taxation did not prevent the plotters from accusing him of doing precisely that when they brought him before Pilate. "We found this fellow perverting the nation," they protested indignantly, "and forbidding to give tribute to Caesar." [21]

It is not surprising that this Tiberius denarius—popularly known as the "tribute penny"—is of all coins the one most in demand by collectors who cherish their New Testaments. Equally sought after, but less commonly found, are counterparts of the "thirty pieces of silver" received by Judas Iscariot for his betrayal of his master. It is true that each fresh rereading of this painful episode is enough to make even the most avid coin collector feel for the moment something of the same disgust for money and its evil power which Judas himself felt later when, in his revulsion against what he had done, "he cast down the pieces of silver . . . and went and hanged himself." [22] Yet despite this disgust there recurs the persistent desire to know precisely what

[20] Matthew 22:15–22.
[21] Luke 23:2.
[22] Matthew 27:5.

those thirty pieces of silver were which purchased one of the greatest betrayals in all history.

This is a question which has been debated for many centuries, and the reasoned answer seems to be that those nefarious pieces were identical with the "large money" with which the chief priests later bribed the Roman soldier-guards to misrepresent the facts of the resurrection. [23] "Large money" was a term commonly used to distinguish large silver coins—usually tetradrachms—from the small silver denarii. The tetradrachms most frequently used in trade in Palestine at this period were (as mentioned earlier) those of Antioch and of Tyre, "idolatrously" adorned with Emperor Augustus on the former and with Melkarth, the Tyrian Baal-worshipers' divinity, on the latter; there can be little doubt that these symbols of man-made deities which every good Jew scorned must have been on the "thirty pieces" which Judas accepted as the price of perfidy and later flung away in horror.

Thirty silver tetradrachms whose monetary value was (to the best of our knowledge) only a little over fifteen dollars in today's American money! For treachery so profound and so far-reaching it was a price minute beyond belief.

[23] *Ibid.*, 28:12–13.

JUDEA: Bronze of Herod Agrippa I, A.D. 41–44.
The obverse bears an umbrella and the Greek inscription "King Agrippa." On the reverse are the
date and three ears of barley.

PARTHIA: Coins of (left) Volagases I, A.D. 51–78, and
(right) Vardanes II, about A.D. 55. The dates overlap because Vardanes as a young prince rebelled against his
father's rule and set up his own régime.

ROME: Dupondius of Augustus, struck presumably at Antioch
about 19–15 B.C. for use in Rome's Eastern lands. "CA" within
the laurel wreath on the reverse stands for "Commune Asiae"
(Commune of Asia).

ASPENDUS (in Pamphylia): Small
bronze of Augustus or Tiberius, about
27 B.C.–A.D. 37. The obverse shows the
head of the emperor; on the reverse are
two cultus statues (objects of worship).

ASPENDUS (in Pamphylia): Silver stater struck
after 300 B.C., with wrestlers on the obverse and
a man wielding a sling on the reverse.

TARSUS: Bronze coin, about 125–100 B.C. The obverse
shows the head of the city; the crown represents city walls.
On the reverse is Sandan, an Oriental god, standing on a
horned and winged lion, with the name of the city in Greek.

THESSALONICA: Bronze, after 88 B.C. The obverse shows the head of the city or a guiding
deity, with the name of the city in Greek. On the
reverse is one of the Cabiri, primitive deities.

CORINTH: Bronze of Caligula, A.D. 37–41, showing Caligula's head on the obverse and Pegasus on the reverse.

EPHESUS: Silver tetradrachm, about 387–295 B.C., bearing two favorite emblems of Ephesus' patron goddess Diana. On the obverse is a bee and on the reverse a stag looking back at a pine tree.

EPHESUS: Silver tetradrachm of Hadrian, A.D. 117–138. On the reverse the many-breasted Ephesian Diana stands between her two stags.

EPHESUS: Reverse of a bronze of Hadrian, A.D. 117–138, showing Diana of Ephesus standing within her temple. This image was believed to have fallen from heaven.

JUDEA: Small bronze of Antonius Felix, Rome's procurator under Claudius and later under Nero; A.D. 54. The obverse bears crossed shields and spears, the reverse a pine tree.

CAESAREA (in Samaria): Bronze coin of Nero, A.D. 67–68. A head of Nero is on the obverse; on the reverse is the goddess of the city, standing with her foot on a ship's prow and holding a ship's standard and a bust of the emperor.

JUDEA: Bronze of Agrippa II, with Emperor Domitian, whose portrait appears on the obverse. Agrippa's name is on the reverse, to the right of a figure of Victory, standing with her foot on a helmet and writing on a shield supported by her left knee. Dated A.D. 86.

ROME: Silver denarius, struck in Sicily (possibly at Syracuse), 38–36 B.C. On the obverse is a head of Pompey the Great; on the reverse is a galley under sail.

PERGAMOS: Cystiferous tetradrachm, about 133–67 B.C.
A mystic cyst, with a snake emerging, is on the obverse; on
the reverse are serpents entwined.

PERGAMOS: Bronze coin of A.D. 14–37, showing on the
obverse a bust of Livia facing a head of Tiberius; on the
reverse is a figure of Augustus standing in a temple.

9

Coins Recalling the Apostles

For the Bible student there is a special interest in the coins which Christ's Apostles must have handled in the course of their tireless evangelical journeys. Since a supply of money was just as necessary to a traveler in that far-off era as it is today, these first century missionaries must undoubtedly have been frequent users of coins native to the many places that they visited.

The difficulty is that any attempt to trace the Apostles' trips numismatically is soon likely to narrow down to an examination of the money known by Paul, for, though we possess odds and ends of information to tell us where the primary bearers of Jesus' message carried on their work, it is for Paul alone that we have a consecutive chronicle. Comparatively few in number are the ancient coins having definite associations with any of the other Apostles.

One of the most significant of these non-Pauline pieces is a small bronze issued a decade after Christ's crucifixion by Herod Agrippa I, a grandson of Herod the Great, who served as Judea's vassal king under the Romans from A.D. 41 to 44. This member of the Herod dynasty, identified as "King Agrippa" in the Greek inscription on the coin pictured here, had in the course of his undistinguished life blundered into various difficulties, including a period of imprisonment for an offense against Tiberius. When he finally did come into power in Judea in late middle age, he was extremely anxious to ingratiate himself with his Jewish subjects, and apparently reasoned that one of the best ways to do so would be to use harsh measures against the disciples of Jesus.

The outstanding episode of his three years on the throne—the episode which makes this coin of his particularly memorable—occurred when "Herod the king stretched forth his hands to vex certain of the church. And he killed James the brother of John with the sword. And . . . he proceeded further to take Peter also. . . . And . . . he put him in prison." [1] The umbrella upon the bronze's obverse, looking to our eyes more like a Christmas tree than like an umbrella, bears mute testimony to the first Agrippa's brief period of supremacy, for the umbrella was an Oriental symbol of power. Gazing at it now, we cannot help wondering whether Peter, escaping from prison through divine intervention, [2] may have carried with him, to help finance his missionary journeys to foreign lands, some replicas of this umbrella-bedecked coin of the puppet king who had persecuted him and had caused the death of his fellow-apostle, James.

Though less definite in apostolic associations than Herod Agrippa's bronze, the oddly shaped money of Parthia (also pictured) seems likely to have been familiar to the disciple Thomas—"doubting Thomas"—who is reputed to have done extensive Christian missionary work among the Parthians in their rugged land southeast of the Caspian Sea during the reigns of the monarchs whom these coins portray. [3] For the most part, though, it must be repeated that to attempt to trace the Apostles' wanderings through coins they knew and used means primarily to trace the journeys

[1] Acts 12:1–4.
[2] *Ibid.,* 12:6–11.
[3] According to the pseudepigraphic Acts of Thomas.

of Paul, who recorded his travels for all posterity. It is true that other Apostles visited and worked in a number of cities, towns, and countries which we have come to associate with Paul. Andrew, for instance, is understood to have spent much time as a missionary in Asia Minor and Macedonia. Yet because his journeys were not so well documented as Paul's, we cannot say with any degree of assurance that Andrew probably handled the coins of such-and-such a place.

With Paul, however, it is a very different matter. In Acts and other books of the New Testament we have such an abundance of geographic references in connection with Paul as to constitute almost an embarrassment of riches. To deal here with the coins of all these places—coins which Paul must surely have encountered—would be an exhausting undertaking. An ambitious and energetic numismatist could spend a lifetime assembling a complete Pauline collection; for our purposes a selected few will suffice.

First of all, there is Antioch, the pioneer center of Christian missions under Paul and Barnabas and the starting point of Paul's three missionary journeys. In this Syrian metropolis, third largest city in the Roman Empire, was struck the Augustan silver tetradrachm described in connection with Judas' ill earned "thirty pieces of silver" at the end of the preceding chapter. Another product believed to have issued from Antioch's mint in this period is the copper dupondius, shown here, which, like the tetradrachm, sought to familiarize the citizens of Rome's Far Eastern provinces with the face of the emperor who was supposed to be worshiped as a deity. Among the Apostles who used these coins with frequency must have been not only Paul and Barnabas, but also Peter, who served for some years as bishop of Antioch's Christian church.

Perhaps one of the most curious of all the facts about the

Antioch of this era was that one of its leading Christian
teachers was Manaen, a foster brother of that very Herod
Antipas who had been so enchanted by Salome's dancing
as to cause the beheading of John the Baptist. [4] This transformation of the Herodian Manaen into a zealous Christian convert was a paradox, certainly, but no more a paradox
than the transformation of the erstwhile jeering Saul of
Tarsus himself.

No longer jeering, but willing to expose himself to the
jeers of others in order to expound the new faith, Paul in
his maiden journey as a missionary, it will be recalled, went
by way of Cyprus to the Roman province of Pamphylia on
the southern coast of Asia Minor. In Pamphylia's port city
of Perga, where he touched twice on this trip in the year
43, he in all likelihood received as change, when he purchased supplies, the small bronzes coined only a few years
before in Aspendus, a bustling nearby Pamphylian city
which boasted one of the world's largest theaters. As may
be seen by the cultus statues on the reverse of this little
coin, the visiting preacher was everywhere confronted by
the entrenched opposition of established and government-
protected religions, and the wonder is not so much that he
occasionally fell afoul of the authorities as that he did not
do so more often.

Because Paul's many references to the winning of races
and similar contests reveal him as interested in sports, it
would be pleasant to believe that he may also have encountered in Pamphylia some of the Aspendian money of an
earlier era—coins featuring athletic designs as appropriate
to his tastes as the pictured silver stater showing wrestlers
and a slinger. Despite the fact that these handsome pieces
were then over three centuries old, it is not beyond the
bounds of possibility that Paul may have seen them during

[4] Acts 13:1.

his Pamphylian visits, for (as has been pointed out before) in ancient days the life of coins was vastly longer than it is today: thanks to their never being called in they often were hoarded for long periods and then put back into use centuries after their original issue.

But if the association of Paul with this old Aspendian stater is admittedly in the realm of wishful thinking, there can be no doubt of his familiarity with the coins of Tarsus, where he is supposed to have touched in the year 49 at the outset of his lengthy second journey. To come to Tarsus was, for Paul, to come home; no matter how long he had been away from his native place, he still was proud to be associated with it. In his crucial hour in Jerusalem he boasted: "I am a man which am a Jew of Tarsus, a city in Cilicia, a citizen of no mean city." [5] The bronze (shown) with its quaint crown of walls and its veneration of an Oriental god must surely have been well known in the childhood of this citizen of Tarsus who was fated to become the foremost apostle of a new faith born in Palestine.

Paul's five-hundred-mile overland journey from Tarsus across Asia Minor to the port of Alexandria Troas (where Luke joined him) took him through many regions reminiscent of landmarks of coinage touched upon in earlier sections of this book. He was a pilgrim in territory where Lydians, Persians, Macedonians, Syrians, and others in their turn had lived and conquered and ruled and declined, leaving ruins—and coins—as their mementos. At Thessalonica, metropolis of the Macedon which had served as the cradle of Alexander the Great, he and his companions lingered for "three sabbath days" [6]—quite long enough, it seems probable, to become well acquainted with the use of a Thessalonican bronze coin very similar to the one of

[5] *Ibid.*, 21:39.
[6] *Ibid.*, 17:2.

Tarsus just described, with the city's guiding patron on one side and its primitive deity on the other.

It was on his way from Thessalonica to Corinth that Paul made the brief stop in Athens which stirred him to deliver his memorable Mars' Hill sermon assailing the Athenians for their idolatry and urging them to forsake their superstitions and to seek and recognize instead "the unknown God."[7] For numismatic enthusiasts it is possible, in all reverence, to agree with this moving appeal of the Apostle's and yet at the same time to be grateful to the "idolatrous" Greeks for the beautiful Athenian tetradrachm and innumerable other exquisite coins (discussed in Chapter 4) which they and their ancestors had created; for the truth is that without such polytheistic portrait galleries, superstitious or no, the realm of ancient coinage would be far less enchanting and picturesque than it is.

How much poorer we should be, for example, if we did not have the charming images of Pegasus, the winged horse, with which the Corinthians for centuries adorned their coinage! The Pegasus on a bronze of Paul's era, it will be noted, has changed somewhat from the one on the Corinthian silver didrachm of the fourth century B.C., but in essence it remains the same. That Paul's fingers must frequently have handled this latter-day Pegasus is a certainty, for during his year and a half's stay in Corinth he not only founded a great church, made many converts, and wrote his first Epistles, but also replenished his purse and supplied his material needs by working at his old trade with Aquila and Priscilla, Jewish tentmakers who had been banished from Italy by Emperor Claudius.[8]

Quite as long-lasting as the cult of Pegasus on Corinth's coinage was that of Diana on the money of Ephesus, the

[7] *Ibid.*, 17:22–23.
[8] *Ibid.*, 18:2–3.

other highly worldly commercial port in which Paul
elected, several years later, to make an extended stay. Ever
since the founding of this thriving city on the Aegean Sea's
eastern shores by Greek colonists some centuries before
Christ, one of the Ephesians' most conspicuous characteris-
tics had been their fanatical worship of the goddess of
natural fertility whom the Greeks called Artemis and the
Romans knew as Diana. The stupendous temple which
they constructed in her honor, requiring more than a century in the building, was included among the seven
wonders of the ancient world, and from the city's earliest
days until long after the time of Paul the coinage of
Ephesus always had Diana and her attributes as its theme.
Thus we range from the famous "bee coin," dating back to
nearly 400 B.C., to the tetradrachms and bronzes of
Hadrian's period, and in all of these, plus an untold number of others which intervened, the Ephesians' emphasis
upon Diana's primacy and divinity is just as persistent as is
the continued refusal of the Jews, during the same period,
to bow their heads to any but their one true God.

It is a remarkable example of Paul's courage that he
should have dared to challenge this dominant national
worship by making Ephesus the center of his missionary
efforts for three years. John, too, lived in Ephesus for a long
period and knew its money well, but of John's stay we have
no such notable reminiscence as was provided by Paul's encounter with the strong hostility of Ephesian silversmiths
and goldsmiths.

This story, told many times before, is worth quoting now
in connection with the coins here reproduced. It reports
that "a certain man named Demetrius, a silversmith, which
made silver shrines for Diana, . . . called together . . . the
workmen of like occupation, and said, Sirs, ye know that
by this craft we have our wealth. Moreover ye see and

hear, that . . . this Paul hath persuaded and turned away much people, saying that they be no gods, which are made with hands: so that not only this our craft is in danger to be set at nought; but also that the temple of the great goddess Diana should be despised, and her magnificence should be destroyed, whom all Asia and the world worshippeth. And when they heard these sayings, they were full of wrath, and cried out, saying, Great is Diana of the Ephesians. And the whole city was filled with confusion." [9]

The threat of potential loss of livelihood which Demetrius pointed out was one which hardheaded businessmen could not disregard, and it had the added menace of encroachment upon established religion. Where would they all be—where, indeed, would the holy Diana herself be—if this interloper Paul should prevail with his talk of Christian doctrines? Should loyal Ephesians stand by unresisting and allow a meddling outlander to belittle the temple and images of Diana (shown here on Hadrian's coins) which had been sacred down through the centuries—the images which were, according to general belief, a direct gift from Jupiter himself?

In this tense moment Paul might very easily have come to grief at the hands of the aroused populace if it had not been for the diplomacy of the town clerk, who "appeased the people," saying: "Ye men of Ephesus, what man is there that knoweth not how that the city of the Ephesians is a worshipper of the great goddess Diana, and of the image which fell down from Jupiter? Seeing then that these things cannot be spoken against, ye ought to be quiet, and to do nothing rashly. . . . And . . . the uproar was ceased." [10]

It seems little less than amazing, in view of the businessmen's enmity and the ordinary Ephesians' passionate and

[9] *Ibid.,* 19:24–29.
[10] *Ibid.,* 19:35–36; 20:1.

long-entrenched devotion to their Heaven-sent Diana, that Paul made as notable progress as he did with the establishing of a Christian church in Ephesus. Probably it was because, as one commentator puts it: "The old faith had little to do with conduct and held out no hopes of future blessedness. . . . The common people were more and more inclining toward . . . Jesus, with his vision of human brotherhood and divine fatherhood. . . . The simple summons 'Come unto me all ye that labor and are heavy laden' proved a mightier power than all the edicts of the emperors." [11]

It was in the year 54, according to most chronologists, that Paul arrived in Ephesus for his three-year-stay. In that very year, which brought the infamous Nero to the Roman throne, a small bronze coin was struck in Palestine by Rome's procurator there, Antonius Felix. Not until five or six years later did Paul, returning to Palestine at last, have his first contact with Felix; and then the design of crossed shields and spears upon the little coin's obverse proved to be a prophetic one: there was to be no peace for the Apostle in the Palestine which Felix ruled.

There is no need to recite here the details of that fateful period nearly nineteen centuries ago when Paul was arrested in Jerusalem on the charge of provoking a riot, given a hearing before this same Felix in the provincial capital at Caesarea, held prisoner there for two years, and then given further hearings before Felix's successor, Festus, and Herod Agrippa II, Judea's vassal king. A new vividness can be added to our understanding of Paul's ordeal during those trying years, however, if we will examine the accompanying coins of Judea under Agrippa and of Caesarea under Nero, and make ourselves realize that these are not merely names on the pages of an oft-read book but are, rather, very real men and places whose active existence

[11] James H. Breasted, *The Conquest of Civilization*, pp. 609–611.

nineteen hundred years ago is attested for us today by well preserved pieces of money which confer a sort of special immortality upon those long-gone rulers and their ruined principalities.

During Festus' governorship no new coins were struck for Palestine; but we need no coins to remind us of that courtroom scene in Caesarea where Paul, after two years as a prisoner, won the new governor's permission to carry his appeal directly to " Caesar" (Nero) in Rome. Nor is a coin of Agrippa necessary (though one does appear here) to bring to mind that equally famous hearing a few days later when this last of the Herodian kings, after listening intently to Paul's presentation of the basis for his religious faith, "said unto Paul, Almost thou persuadest me to be a Christian." [12]

"Almost!" Though Herod Agrippa II lived to be an old man, and held Judea's throne for over fifty years, the single word "almost" is surely the best remembered and most meaningful that he ever spoke.

Of Paul's subsequent eventful voyage to Rome, under guard, the pictured denarius of Sicily, where he spent three days at Syracuse, is an appropriate memento because the galley shown on its reverse is in all probability a replica of the ones in which he and his fellow prisoners made that storm-tossed journey under the guardianship of Julius, the centurion. The few remaining years of the Great Apostle's life and work are tied up closely with the Rome of Nero, which is represented for us by the sestertius of that profligate ruler portrayed with the next chapter.

In suffering martyrdom during the persecution of Christians under Nero, Paul was not, of course, alone among the Apostles, for Peter is generally believed to have met his death under similar auspices on the same day. Yet it is of interest to note, in skimming through the portrait gallery of

[12] Acts 26:28.

Roman emperors of New Testament years in the following chapter, that at least one of these emperors, Nerva, whose reign occurred nearly thirty years after Nero's disgrace and suicide, altered most refreshingly the established pattern of imperial Christian baiting. Nerva it was who, in the year 96, liberated the aged Apostle John from his banishment on the island of Patmos in the Aegean Sea and permitted him to return to Ephesus, where he had lived before and where, like Paul, he doubtless was forced to make use of coins honoring the Ephesian Diana even while his thoughts and labors were devoted to the spreading of Christianity.

For John, however, as for all the other early Christian teachers, this was no novel experience. Of John's wanderings and stopping places, to be sure, we have no such definite information as we have of Paul's, but we do know that one of his concerns in the book of Revelation is with the continuing struggle between the Christian church at Pergamos and "Satan's seat" in that thriving city of Asia Minor. [13] What John called "Satan's seat" was the mystic cyst which was kept in the Asclepium, the magnificent temple at Pergamos dedicated to the worship of Asclepius, the god of medicine whose name has come down to us in its Roman form: Aesculapius. This mystic cyst, shown in all its original clarity on the tetradrachm of Pergamos pictured here, was a chest wherein was kept a live serpent which was a special object of veneration for all devout Asclepians. As may be observed, the designers of the cystiferous tetradrachm, not content with the partial glimpse of the serpent peering from the cyst which the coin's obverse affords, have embellished the reverse with two such serpents intricately entwined, thus presenting the forerunner of the caduceus which is used until this day as a medical symbol.

In all likelihood some of the serpent-adorned tetra-

[13] Revelation 2:13.

drachms representing "Satan's seat" were still in use in Pergamos even in John's day, but for everyday purposes they had been replaced by more conventional coins such as the bronze of the period of Tiberius, shown here, on which the likeness of Rome's second emperor is confronted by one of Livia, his mother. Perhaps the most significant thing about this coin is its reverse, where the figure of Augustus is portrayed standing in a temple. In short, John might have a loyal band of Christian followers at Pergamos, but control of the temples, as of the currency, was firmly in the hands of the Roman emperors, with a colorful mythology built around the gods of Mount Olympus and around their own supposed divinity. In tracing the coins bearing upon the Christian church's development, it is to these emperors, therefore, that we now must turn.

ROME: Silver denarius of Augustus, 27 B.C.–A.D. 14. The reverse shows Pax (Peace) holding an olive branch and cornucopias.

ROME: Bronze as, struck in A.D. 10–11, showing Tiberius as a young prince under Augustus. (Tiberius's own reign was A.D. 14–37.) The "SC" on the reverse—a common inscription on Roman coins—stands for "Senatus consulto" (with consent of the Senate).

ROME: Sestertius of Caligula, A.D. 37–41. On the reverse Caligula is addressing soldiers.

119

ROME: Sestertius of Claudius, A.D. 41–54. On the reverse is Spes (Hope).

ROME: Sestertius of Nero, A.D. 54–68. The triumphal arch on the reverse is probably the one erected by Nero during the Parthian War.

ROME: Sestertius of Galba (A.D. 68–69) with Winged Victory on the reverse.

ROME: Silver denarius of Otho, A.D. 69. The figure on the reverse, holding a wreath and a scepter, is "Securitas" (Confidence or Security).

ROME: Sestertius of Vitellius, A.D. 69. The reverse presents impersonations of Honor (here obliterated) and Courage.

JUDEA: Bronze, period of First Revolt, A.D. 66–70, showing a diota (wine jar) on the obverse and a vine leaf on the reverse.

JUDEA: Silver half-shekel, formerly believed to have been made at the time of Simon Maccabee, but now generally credited to the period of the First Revolt, A.D. 66–70. On the obverse is a chalice or pot of manna; the inscription reads "Half-shekel Israel." On the reverse is a blossoming rod; the inscription says "Jerusalem the Holy."

ROME: Sestertius of Vespasian (A.D. 69–79), struck in the year 71 to commemorate the conquest of Judea, depicted on the reverse by a mourning Jewess seated under a palm tree, with the emperor in military garb behind her, and the words "Judaea Capta" at the sides.

ROME: Denarius showing Titus (emperor A.D. 79–81), struck during the reign of Vespasian. The reverse, like that of Vespasian's sestertius, celebrates the capture of Judea and is similar in design.

ROME: Sestertius of Domitian, A.D. 81–96, struck in the last year of his reign. The reverse depicts the emperor at the altar clasping hands with a general accompanied by two soldiers.

ROME: Sestertius of Nerva A.D. 96–98, commemorating, in almost illegible inscription on the reverse, Nerva's "removal of the scandal of the Jewish tax." The palm tree symbolizes Judea.

10

Portraits from New Testament Years

During the slightly more than a hundred years covered by the New Testament—the years from 6 B.C. to A.D. 96— twelve emperors held sway in Rome. Innumerable tribunes, consuls, senators, procurators, generals, and other officials functioned under these monarchs, of course, but the emperors wielded power so sweeping that in the pages of history theirs are the names which have survived. Especially true is this for the numismatist, for in the days of the empire the vast majority of Rome's coins were portraits of its royal rulers.

Because the actions and policies of these rulers had such lasting effects upon the fortunes of both Christians and Jews, the collector who enjoys acquiring coins of Biblical significance will find particular fascination in trying to assemble a full portrait gallery of this imperial twelve, ranging from Augustus (whose long reign ended with his death in A.D. 14) through Tiberius (14–37), Caligula (37–41), Claudius (41–54), Nero (54–68), Galba (68–69), Otho (69), Vitellius (69), Vespasian (69–79), Titus (79–81), and Domitian (81–96), and ending with Nerva (96–98).

You cannot hope to find all twelve at once, of course, but, as in building up any type of collection, you *can* hope to pick them up one by one. It goes almost without saying that the foresighted collector will not necessarily try to assemble his emperors in chronological order, beginning with

Augustus and working his way down the line. Instead he will begin with whichever one he can get, and hope that later on, with luck and persistence, he may be able to find the others.

The most popular denomination among these imperial portraits, because of its giant size, is the bronze sestertius, the coin of four-as value which is also commonly known as the "large brass" or "large bronze." (The other principal Roman coins of this period, in addition to the bronze as, were the silver denarius, worth about four times as much as the sestertius, and the bronze dupondius of half-sestertius value.) Despite its generous proportions the sestertius had a monetary value rather less than that of the American nickel, so of course it was in extremely common usage and must have served to buy food and drink for many a secret Christian or exiled Jew. But it is not possible to have a complete New Testament set of these large likenesses, for no regal portrait ever appeared on sestertii of Augustus, Tiberius, or Otho. Often, moreover, a small coin in fine condition may be a more desirable possession than a large coin of worn or battered aspect.

It may be helpful here to insert a few words about the inscriptions on these imperial Roman coins. Many a would-be collector, observing the apparently meaningless jumbles of letters with which the emperors' heads usually are encircled, gives up as hopeless any attempt to decipher these inscriptions. Such faintheartedness is unfortunate, for actually the interpreting of the legends is not nearly so complicated as it appears.

The chief difficulty is that Rome's moneyers had a consuming passion for abbreviations and a bland disregard of the need for placing any dots or spaces between these abbreviated words. But a very little study will show that to make up for these irritating habits they used the same abbreviations over and over again: COS for consul, IMP for imperator (emperor), TRP for tribunician power, AUG for Augustus and CAES for Caesar (both of these being used, eventually, more as titles than as part of the emperors' names), PM for pontifex maximus (high priest), PP for pater patriae (father of his country), and so on down the line. Once these oft-repeated abbreviations are understood, the previously obscure hodgepodge of letters begins to take on clarity and meaning.

To demonstrate the comparative ease of deciphering these capitals, let us examine two typical sestertii: those of Claudius and of Domitian pictured with this chapter. With a good magnifying glass it is possible to make out nearly all of the letters on these photographs. (And here a warning may be offered: in order to decipher these inscriptions more easily collectors should never make the error of cleaning the centuries-old coating of patina from ancient coins, for in the opinion of experts this patina adds greatly to a coin's charm and value.)

On Claudius's coin, reading clockwise and starting at the bottom center, we find TICLAVDIVSCAESARAVGPMT RPIMP. Broken down into its component parts, and with the abbreviations spelled out, this reads: Tiberius Claudius, Caesar Augustus, Pontifex Maximus (high priest), Tribunicia Potestate (holder of the tribune's power, that is, supreme head of the nation), Imperator (emperor).

The legend on the obverse of Domitian's sestertius (some of it nearly obliterated in this version) is: IMPCAESDO MITAVGGERMCOSX (next letter or figure illegible, but probably V) IIICENSPERPP. Certainly this appears formidable at first glance, but with only the most rudimentary knowledge of common abbreviations we can provide the necessary translation: Imperator Caesar Domitian Augustus Germanicus ("Germanicus" was a title of honor),

Consul XVIII (in his eighteenth consulship), Censor Per-
petuus (perpetual chief magistrate), Pater Patriae (father of
his country).

It is a miracle of condensation, certainly, to encompass
so much information in so small a space, and for the collector one of the most valuable aspects of such an inscription is that the numerals which frequently follow the TRP,
the IMP, and the COS (as with the COSXVIII on this
sestertius of Domitian) make it possible in many cases to
determine the exact date of the coin. [1]

"But what," the collector may ask, "do all these Roman
emperors have to do with the Bible?" With the Bible itself,
it is true, their connection is slight, but for those to whom
the Bible is important they are significant for two reasons.
First, the coins bearing their imperial likenesses were the
ones used in daily life and trade by the early Christians
and by the many Jews who were scattered in all parts of
the Roman world. And, second, the emperors are significant
because a number of them made a practice of persecuting
both Jews and Christians, thereby rendering a service to
those whom they sought to destroy, for in the spreading
and strengthening of religious devotion nothing seems to be
more effective than persecution.

Not all of the twelve can be accused of oppressing these
religious groups. There was Augustus, for instance, who
lived too soon to be confronted with the phenomenon of
Christianity, but who played such an important if indirect
part (as recalled at the end of Chapter Seven) in the events
preceding Christ's birth, when "there went out a decree
from Caesar Augustus that all the world should be taxed." [2]

[1] Just how this determination is made is too technical a matter to be covered in
a work of this sort. An invaluable treatment of the subject will be found in Zander
H. Klawans's *Reading and Dating Roman Imperial Coins* (Whitman Publishing Co.,
Racine, Wis., 1953).

[2] Luke 2:1.

The pictured denarius of the first Roman emperor is one of singular clarity and beauty, so perfect in its preservation as to make almost incredible the realization that nearly two millenniums have passed since its minting.

The as portraying Tiberius which follows the denarius of his stepfather, Augustus, reminds us of the role played in the New Testament by this second of Rome's emperors, who reigned throughout the period of Christ's ministry. Luke refers to him by name,[3] and he was the "Caesar" of whom Jesus was speaking when he said "Render . . . unto Caesar the things which are Caesar's."[4]

The letters "SC" (meaning that the Senate has been consulted), appearing on the reverse of this as of Tiberius and on many other Roman coins, bear witness to the empire's theoretical provision that the striking of all coins except gold ones was authorized by the Senate, rather than by the emperor. In practice, however, the emperor was usually supreme and minted whatever coins he desired.

If, as suggested earlier, the sestertius is the most coveted of the imperial portrait-bearing coins of the New Testament period, it is ironic that the first one on the list should belong to Caligula, the third emperor, a madman whose four-year record of depravity, extravagance, and cruelty is one of the very blackest of the many dark spots in the empire's checkered history.

This monarch's chief claim to the attention of Bible students is that it was he who took Herod Agrippa I out of prison (where Tiberius had confined him) and placed him in authority in Judea. Despite his almost uninterrupted orgies of debauchery and barbarism, Caligula's treatment of both the Christians and the Jews was less abusive than was that of many of his successors, possibly because, in his

[3] *Ibid.*, 3:1.
[4] Matthew 22:21.

insanity, he was not capable of distinguishing such fine points as the religion of his victims. Members of his family, officers of his legions—who they were made no difference when the murderous fury was upon him, and it is not surprising that his disastrous reign ended with his own murder by a soldier. (And who could possibly prove us wrong if we should choose to assume that the tyrant's assassin was one of the very soldiers whom he is shown addressing on the reverse of the sestertius pictured here?)

Surprisingly enough there is a marked similarity between the coin-borne portrait of the mad Caligula and that of his somewhat weak but generally well disposed uncle, Claudius, who succeeded him. Claudius was, like Caligula, a friend of Judea's Herod Agrippa I, and, more than that, he has the distinction of being mentioned by name twice in the Bible: first in connection with the prophecy of Agabus concerning famine in Syria and Palestine, [5] and second for his edict banishing the Jews from Rome. [6]

His importance to Bible students, however, lies not so much in these New Testament references as in the fact that he was the first Roman emperor to observe and become alarmed at the spread of the new sect called Christians, the followers of an obscure Judean who had been crucified during the reign of Tiberius. His alarm was augmented by the dissensions which kept flaring up between Christians and Jews, and it was in the hope that there would be less trouble if the two sects were separated that he issued his decree expelling Jews from the city of Rome. It was this act of Claudius which sent the Jewish-born tentmakers Aquila and Priscilla to Corinth, where their association with Paul gave their names immortality.

But any concern which Claudius may have felt at the

[5] Acts 11:28.
[6] *Ibid.*, 18:2.

growth of the Christian movement was as nothing compared to that which moved his ill famed stepson, Nero, to some of the notable excesses of brutality which will be forever associated with his name. The startling contrast between Nero's bull-like profile and the slim, patrician features of his predecessors is no greater than is the contrast between his record of calculated cruelty and the statesmanlike moderation of Augustus, Tiberius (in his earlier years), and Claudius. Probably it never will be known whether or not Nero was responsible for the great fire which destroyed a large part of Rome during his reign, but there can be little doubt that, whatever the cause of the fire, it was the emperor himself who was largely responsible for making the Christians the scapegoats. Doubtless he thought that by spreading rumors that the Christians were guilty he was distracting attention from suspicions of his own complicity. More than that, however, he was really worried at the strength which the once despised and ignored Christian community had achieved. Throughout the empire their numbers had been expanding steadily.

The thing about this expansion which particularly disturbed Nero and his supporters was that these upstarts, though peaceable enough, absolutely refused to offer divine honors to the emperors. The way to eliminate this Christian nuisance and this impious disrespect for his sacred person, Nero seems to have reasoned, was to eliminate the Christians themselves. Hence he accused them of having burned the city, and proceeded to execute them in great numbers. Of some he made torches, having them wrapped in pitch-impregnated cloth and burned by night. Some were crucified; some were sewn into animal skins and thrown to dogs to be torn to pieces.

It was during this carnival of horror that Paul and Peter presumably perished, the former being beheaded outside

the city gates, the latter being crucified, head down, upon
the site known as "Nero's Circus," which is now just in
front of the entrance of St. Peter's Church in Rome. That
Paul should have met his end in this fashion is especially
ironic when it is recalled that Nero was the authority in
whom he had placed his trust when he said to Festus, "I
stand at Caesar's judgment seat," and, "I appeal unto
Caesar," [7] and whom Festus meant when he agreed that
"unto Caesar shalt thou go," [8] and later explained to King
Herod Agrippa that Paul "hath appealed to Augustus." [9]

In making martyrs of Peter and Paul and countless other
Christians in order to distract people from his own short-
comings, Nero set a pattern which was to be followed by
his successors for several centuries. Whenever the empire's
fortunes seemed to be waning, persecutions of scapegoat
Christians recurred as regularly as did persecutions of Jews
by the Nazis in modern times.

In Nero's case, however, the campaign against the Christians was not enough to keep him in favor. His excesses,
combined with a series of military and other disasters, had
made him widely hated, and when the generals of his legions rose in insurrection he committed suicide. With his
death there came to an end the line of the Caesars, whether
direct or adoptive. From then on "Caesar" was no longer
the emperor's family name, but a title—a title which was
supposed to possess a divine significance and which continued throughout the years to appear on coins.

Of the three emperors who immediately followed this
last of the Caesars, there is little to say from the viewpoint
of the Bible, of numismatics, or of history itself. In the widespread confusion following Nero's suicide three generals

[7] *Ibid.*, 25:10, 11.
[8] *Ibid.*, 25:12.
[9] *Ibid.*, 25:25.

who were briefly successful claimants to the throne—Galba, Otho, and Vitellius—came and went in less than a year. The marvel is that they had time to strike coins to commemorate their short reigns, but the illustrations testify that they did.

Then came yet a fourth general, Vespasian, whose rise to the throne was due largely to his popularity with the soldiers who had been serving under him in Palestine, where he had been trying to put down the revolt of the Jews. This revolt had started in the year 66, during Nero's reign, while Gessius Florus was procurator of Judea. Throughout the years of Roman overlordship there had been many humiliations to try the pride and patience of the Jews, but the last straw had been the Romans' plundering of seventeen talents—a vast amount—from the temple's treasure. (A silver talent, it will be remembered, was worth over $1,600 in our money; the value of a golden talent was more than $26,000.)

At this crowning indignity the Jews rose in revolt under the leadership of Eleazar, captain of the temple, who was a son of Ananias, the high priest with whom the Apostle Paul had come in conflict. In short order the aroused Judeans massacred the entire Roman garrison and then proceeded to hold their beloved Jerusalem against the attempts of Cestius Gallus, Roman governor of Syria, to reclaim it for the empire.

For the moment, the tiny Jewish nation was triumphant against the forces of the great Roman empire, enjoying freedom from outside domination for the first time since the days of the Maccabees. Nero had promptly sent Vespasian and his legions to quell the uprising, but it refused to be downed without a long and violent struggle.

Meanwhile the resurgent Jews helped to celebrate their precarious independence by issuing their own money. There

were some (probably not more than two) little bronzes—
delicate diota-and-vine-leaf-adorned slivers, one of which is
reproduced here. But the most memorable coins of this four-
year period of revolt are the silver ones, generally believed
to have been the first silver money ever issued by the
Jews. [10] Now, more than two centuries after the Syrian King
Antiochus VII had given Simon Maccabee "leave to coin
money for thy country with thine own stamp," [11] reborn
Judea at last had silver pieces of its own—pieces which it
proudly called "shekels" in honor of the ancient Hebrew
unit of weight. There were half- and quarter-shekels, too
(the half is pictured here), all bearing types or designs sub-
stantially similar to that of the silver shekel itself: on the
obverse the pot of manna which Moses had counseled
Aaron to lay before the Lord, [12] and on the reverse, encircled by the words "Jerusalem the Holy," a branch with
three blossoms—presumably Aaron's rod which "brought
forth buds, and bloomed blossoms, and yielded almonds." [13]

For many years the Children of Israel had been forced to
use in their daily dealings the silver denarii of Rome, the
silver tetradrachms of such Greek-inspired strongholds as
Antioch and Tyre, and the bronze coins of the Roman procurators and of Judea's vassal kings, the Herods, despite the
fact that many of these coins bore the heads of successive
Roman emperors—the "graven images" against which the
Jews had been cautioned by God. [14] Now at last, if only for
a limited time, they had coinage—even silver coinage—of
their own design. These pieces, though markedly inferior
in workmanship to the output of the skilled moneyers of

---

[10] See Chap. 6 for a discussion of former attribution of silver coinage to Simon
Maccabee.

[11] I Maccabees 15:6.

[12] Exodus 16:33.

[13] Numbers 17:8.

[14] Exodus 20:4.

Antioch and Rome, are symbolic of the exalted desperation of that four-year period during which even the most fanatical of the Jewish rebels must have known that defeat was inevitable.

The defeat came in the year 70, only a few months after Vespasian had returned to Rome to claim the throne, leaving his son Titus to complete the subjugation of Judea. Even then the fall of Judea was due as much to famine as to force of arms; prolonged siege by Titus and his legions had left the people of the city without food, though they now had money of their own coinage with which to buy it. For half-starved men they defended their stronghold with amazing tenacity, losing over a hundred thousand of their members in the process.

Nearly as many again, having been compelled to witness the agonizing sight of the burning, looting, and total destruction of their sacred temple, were taken in slavery, many of them being forced—like the Christians of their era—to serve as doomed gladiators or as helpless quarries for wild beasts in the spectacular "sports" which the triumphant Titus staged at Caesarea Philippi to celebrate his victory. [15] (King Herod Agrippa II, it is worthy of note, did not suffer the gruesome fate of his subjects; as befitted a puppet king who always had faithfully displayed the current Roman emperor's likeness on his coins, he was allowed to retire to Rome in comfort, to live out the rest of his long life with the rank and dignity of a magistrate.)

These gladiatorial shows were only one small part of the frenzy of celebration into which the Roman Empire plunged after its conquest of little Judea. For some years imperial Rome had been starved for military victories, and now the putting down of the Jewish revolt provided a much

[15] Jerusalem's conquest, the temple's destruction, and the Jews' being "led away captive into all nations" were prophesied by Jesus in Matthew 24:2 and Luke 21:24.

needed salve to pride. It is true that the match was a most
unequal one and that the victory required a long time to
achieve, but that did not prevent the Flavian emperors (as
Vespasian and his sons are called) from making it the
cornerstone of their régimes.

Thus it was that in the year 71 the emperor and his sons
Titus and Domitian all took part in a mammoth march of
triumph to celebrate Jerusalem's destruction. Carried as
trophies through the streets of Rome were the temple's
precious seven-branched candlestick, its golden table of
shewbread, and its silver trumpets. More enduring than
any parades or festivals were the numerous "victory" coins,
struck both in Palestine and at Rome. Typical of these is
the sestertius of Vespasian pictured here, with its reverse
showing the exultant emperor, the inscription "Judaea
Capta," and the weeping Jewess whom Isaiah apparently
had envisioned eight centuries before when he had prophesied "and she being desolate shall sit upon the ground." [16]

Not only Vespasian, but Titus too, was honored in the
long series of coins rejoicing in Rome's subjugation of
Judea, as can be seen from the illustrated denarius of Titus,
which has a reverse almost exactly like that of the Vespasian
sestertius. These are only two out of at least twenty-odd
coins by which over a long period the first two Flavian
emperors sought never to let their subjects forget that they
had been responsible for the glorious capture of tiny Judea.

Even Domitian, who succeeded to his brother's throne a
full eleven years after Jerusalem's fall, continued on some
of his coins to stress this theme, although the sestertius of
Domitian illustrated in these pages happens instead to
show the last of the three Flavian emperors in the process
of exchanging a friendly handclasp with one of his generals.
This pose of amity with the army has its highly ironic as-

[16] Isaiah 3:26.

pects, in view of the fact that Domitian (unlike his father and brother) was a cruel tyrant patterned after Caligula and Nero—a tyrant so bitterly resented by his army officers that, less than a year after this coin's minting, one of them murdered him.

Like Nero in his choice of scapegoats, as well as in his despotism, Domitian followed up his family's efforts at exterminating the Jews by trying to do likewise with the Christians. One of the highlights of his efforts in this direction was his treatment of John, whom he chose not to kill but to banish to the Isle of Patmos, where this last-remaining of Jesus' disciples is believed to have written Revelation.

With the Jews, too—who, despite all attempts, had stubbornly refused to be wiped out—Domitian made his reign felt by enforcing with the most humiliating methods the collecting of the tribute tax, which had been in effect even in the days of Jesus [17] and which after the Revolt (according to Josephus) "Caesar . . . laid upon the Jews wheresoever they were, and enjoined every one of them to bring two drachmae every year into the Capitol, as they used to pay the same to the temple at Jerusalem." [18]

Domitian's insulting tactics aroused the Jews to such a high pitch of resentment that after his assassination his successor, Nerva (whom the Senate chose as Rome's new emperor), determined to make amends. He did not entirely abolish the tribute tax itself, but he did do away with the obnoxious system of false accusations which formerly had been employed in its collection. Numismatic evidence of this reform is the sestertius of Nerva illustrated here, which bears on its reverse the inscription: "Removal of the scandal of the Jewish tax."

So grateful were the Jews for this at least partial release

[17] Matthew 22:17–21.
[18] Josephus, *Wars of the Jews*, Bk. VII, Chap. 6.

from the indignities under which they had suffered that they came to look upon Nerva as their friend and benefactor. To show their appreciation they adopted a method which is a coin collector's delight: they took whatever coins of the hated Domitian they had in their possession and countermarked them with a head of Nerva! Today such tampering with a coin might send one to jail, but nineteen hundred years ago the official attitude toward coins of the realm must have been more indulgent, for many of these Domitian-supplanted-by-Nerva pieces have been found in Samaria and Judea. [19]

With the short reign of the beneficent Nerva the New Testament years came to a close. During those years the young fellowship of Christianity had grown from nothing at all to impressive proportions. Its insistent spread within the Roman Empire, in the face of danger, bans, and official persecution, was a symptom of the weakness which in time would wreck the empire. The slaves and common people, dissatisfied with their lot, craved a religion and a way of life which would give them hope and dignity. Emperors might proclaim on coins and elsewhere that they were divine, but their subjects had other ideas as to divinity—ideas which the doctrines of Christianity seemed to bring closer to realization. Yet more than two centuries were to pass before the emperors would finally perceive this craving and bow to the inevitable, leaving in their coinage a clear-cut record of their surrender.

[19]Authority for this is E. Rogers' *A Handy Guide to Jewish Coins* (Spink and Son, London, 1914), pp. 49–50.

ROME: Sestertius of Hadrian (A.D. 117–138), struck in 132–134. On the reverse is a ship moving eastward.

JUDEA: Silver shekel of the Second Revolt (A.D. 132–135), overstruck on a tetradrachm of Antioch. The obverse, bearing Simon's name, shows the Tabernacle with the Ark of the Covenant inside. On the reverse are a lulab (bundle of twigs) and an ethrog (citron) at left, with the encircling inscription "Second year of the Deliverance of Jerusalem."

JUDEA: Overstruck copper coin of the Second Revolt, A.D. 132–135. The obverse bears a vine leaf and the inscription "Deliverance of Jerusalem"; on the reverse are a palm tree and Simon's name.

ROME: Denarius of Hadrian, A.D. 117–138. The figure on the reverse is Equity, or Justice, holding scales and a horn of plenty.

139

JUDEA: Silver quarter-shekel of the Second Revolt (A.D. 132–135), overstruck on a Roman denarius. On the obverse are a bunch of grapes and the name "Simon" (for Simon Bar Cocheba, the revolt leader). On the reverse is a lyre, with the inscription "Deliverance of Jerusalem."

NEAPOLIS IN SAMARIA: Sestertius of Antoninus Pius (A.D. 138–161) showing, on the reverse, the Temple of Jupiter on Mount Gerizim.

ROME: As of Marcus Aurelius, struck in A.D. 177. The galley on the reverse, with Neptune standing in the stern, commemorates the emperor's safe return from his Eastern campaign.

ROME: Denarius of Diocletian (emperor A.D. 284–305), struck at Londinium (London) about A.D. 300. The reverse depicts a sacrifice before the city gate.

ROME: Bronze follis (A.D. 295–306), showing Constantine I (Constantine the Great) as prince before he ascended the throne. On the reverse, in military dress, he is holding two standards.

ROME: Small bronze, struck between A.D. 335 and 337 by Constantine the Great, showing Helena, ardent Christian and mother of Constantine. The figure on the reverse is that of Pax (Peace), holding an olive branch and a scepter.

ROME: Christian symbol (labarum) on the reverse of a follis of Magnentius (A.D. 350–353).

11

Judea's End and
Christian Rome's Beginning

By rights, perhaps, this book should end with the preceding chapter, which brings to a close the "Bible Days" of the title. Yet in order to round out numismatically the Bible's two dominant themes—the Jewish people's struggle for their homeland and the birth and triumphal growth of the Christian movement—there is a strong temptation to carry on just a little further. Certainly it is beyond our province to trace the treatment of Judaism and Christianity by each of Rome's emperors in turn, but the two historic events mentioned in this chapter's heading cannot be neglected.

Judea's end? Vespasian and Titus thought that they had accomplished it in A.D. 70, but they reckoned without the remarkable recuperative power of a people who, however tortured and dispersed, remained united; they and their successors failed to take into account the massive force which smoldering resentment can beget.

The period of Hadrian (A.D. 117–138) is generally considered one of the high points of the Roman Empire, yet it was during Hadrian's reign that the Second Revolt of the Jews occurred. It was unthinkable that the Jews could revolt again only threescore years after Jerusalem had been destroyed and its people scattered "from the one end of the earth even unto the other." [1] Nevertheless, revolt they did; and, as in their earlier period of rebellion, they were for several years so successful as to revive a semblance of their independent nation, complete with that most enduring of all attributes of national sovereignty, their own coinage.

The sestertius of Hadrian pictured here, featuring on its reverse his galley moving eastward, may indirectly have had something to do with the inception of that revolt. Hadrian paid triumphal visits to all parts of his empire, and when he made one of these journeys to Palestine in A.D. 131 or 132 he was ill advised enough not only to forbid observance of the Jewish Sabbath and performance of the rite of circumcision, but also—crowning indignity—to announce plans for building a new Roman colony, featuring a temple to Jupiter, on the site of Jerusalem and its lamented temple. News of this impending desecration was just the spark needed to precipitate the revolt which followed.

Leader of the insurrection was Simon Bar Cocheba, known variously to history as Bar Cocheba, Barcochab, Bar Cochba, Bar Kozba, and Bar Koziba. His name, however spelled, meant "son of a star," and he claimed to be the long-expected Messiah, basing his claim on Balaam's prophecy: "There shall come a Star out of Jacob, and a Sceptre shall rise out of Israel." [2] Raising an army of 200,000 followers in open defiance of Roman sovereignty, he quickly gained possession of many strongholds and villages, and although Rome sent one of its ablest generals to quell the revolt it was more than three years before the defiant Jews could be forced to surrender, losing both their bid for independence and a catastrophic number of lives.

In the period before this tragic climax, however, the reborn nation produced a vast quantity of memorable coins.

[1] Deuteronomy 28:64.
[2] Numbers 24:17.

From the numismatic point of view, in fact, the Second Revolt is the most interesting period of all Jewish history. Scorning to use the money of their enemies in its original form, the rebels overstruck with characteristically Judean dies any coins they could get hold of. They *had* to use these old coins as the fabric for their new ones, for they no longer had any ingots of precious metal of their own, all the temple's treasure having been seized by the Romans at the time of the First Revolt.

Because they were hard-pressed for time and inexpert at the moneyer's art, much of the overstriking was extremely careless. Aesthetically, this is no doubt unfortunate, but as an aid in latter-day detective work it is invaluable. On many a hastily overstruck coin parts of the type and legend of the original still are visible—so much so, that sometimes the defaced coin can be identified. They particularly delighted in obliterating the portraits and titles of Rome's emperors, deriving what one numismatic authority has called a "savage satisfaction in this effacement of the hated image and superscription of Caesar." [3]

Now once again, as in their earlier insurrection, the embattled Jews were able to have as their most valuable pieces of money not the tetradrachms of foreign powers but silver shekels of their own fabricating. To make these they simply altered the tetradrachms of nearby Antioch and Tyre—particularly those of Antioch. They overstruck so many, in fact, that we begin to understand why it is so difficult to find any of the unaltered original silver coins of Antioch when we are seeking specimens of the "thirty pieces of silver" by which Judas was bribed. [4] On the obverse, in place of Augustus' head, went a picture of the entrance to the Holy of Holies, with its four pillars of shittim wood

[3] E. Rogers, *A Handy Guide to Jewish Coins*, p. 52.
[4] See Chap. 8.

overlaid with gold, and, within the entrance, the ark and the mercy seat, all as specified by the Lord to Moses.[5] Above the Holy of Holies on some of these silver shekels, but not upon them all, there is a star—Bar Cocheba's symbol. On the reverse, supplanting Antioch's Tyche, are the lulab and citrons which we encountered on Judean copper pieces back in the days of the Maccabees.[6]

Smaller silver pieces were overstruck too, as well as coppers, but the coin which was most needed, the half-shekel (required for sacred tribute), seldom could be made, for it had to be counterstruck on a didrachm, and didrachms were extremely rare. Hence the Jews of the Second Revolt period used two denarii, transformed by overstriking into quarter-shekels, for their temple tribute money. Thus the silver denarius of Hadrian (pictured) became a Jewish quarter-shekel like the one shown here, with the royal features replaced by a bunch of grapes and the figure of Justice supplanted by a lyre. In similar fashion the denarii of other Roman rulers were overstruck to fill the pressing need for quarter-shekels.

Hebrew inscriptions on practically all these monetary pieces of the Second Revolt give the dates of "the deliverance of Israel" or "the deliverance of Jerusalem." Some bear the name "Simon" or "Simeon" (for Bar Cocheba), while some are marked "Eleazar the Priest."

After the revolt had been brought to an end by the slaughter of almost the entire Jewish population, Hadrian went ahead with his interrupted plans to build on Jerusalem's site a new Roman city, which he called Aelia Capitolina in honor of his family name, Aelius; and within this city, on the site of the Jews' beloved temple, he erected the dreaded temple to Jupiter. Inasmuch as the Jews were

[5] Exodus 26:32, 34.
[6] See Chap. 6.

forbidden even to enter this new colony, they were crushingly deprived at last of their cherished Holy City—a deprivation which lasted for more than 1,800 years.

Only a few years after this blackest of all black periods in Hebrew history there came into being a most unusual sestertius commemorating another holy place of the Jews: Mount Gerizim. For this coin, so exceptionally rich in Biblical associations, we are indebted to Hadrian's successor, Antoninus Pius. Centuries before the sestertius in question was struck, Mount Gerizim had come to be associated not so much with the Jews as with the Samaritans, who, claiming that the mountain was the original site of the Garden of Eden, had built their temple upon its peak to rival that of the Jews at Jerusalem. Yet, whatever schisms the Hebrews might have had with the Samaritans, they never could disregard the claims which this sacred site had upon their own tribal memories, for it was there or near there that Abraham had built his first altar,[7] that Joshua had written upon stones a copy of the law of Moses,[8] and that Jotham had stood while he told his "Fable of the Trees."[9]

More than that, Jacob's well was near the foot of Mount Gerizim, where (as Christians will recall) Jesus rested and talked with the woman of Samaria while his disciples went into the city to buy meat.[10] "Our fathers worshipped in this mountain,"[11] the Samaritan woman told Jesus, and Mount Gerizim as a site of worship is precisely what Antoninus Pius's coin portrays.

At this point, however, it must be admitted that the temple shown on the sestertius is not the one where devout

[7] Genesis 12:6, 7.
[8] Joshua 8:32, 33.
[9] Judges 9:7–15.
[10] John 4:5–9. Here the city of Shechem (later Neapolis) is spoken of as "Sychar," presumably a variation of Sychem, the Greek form for Shechem.
[11] *Ibid.*, 4:20.

Samaritans had worshiped, for that had been destroyed in
120 B.C. by John Hyrcanus, one of Judea's Maccabean
rulers. The shrine on Gerizim preserved in likeness by this
coin is, to be sadly frank, neither a Jewish nor a traditional
Samaritan place of worship, but the Temple of Jupiter
which had been built by Hadrian to serve the people of the
neighboring city which, under the Emperor Vespasian, had
lost its ancient Biblical name of Shechem, becoming known
as Neapolis instead. The grandiose staircase for which that
Temple of Jupiter was famed gives the appearance in this
reproduction of running all the way from the bottom of the
mountain to the top, but we can forgive that touch of exaggeration because of the welcome service the coin performs
in bringing us a vivid memento of the scene of so many
Biblical events.

The monarch portrayed on the Gerizim bronze's obverse,
Antoninus Pius, was rare among the members of the imperial line in that he was willing to tolerate and protect the
troublesome Christians who were such a thorn in the flesh
of the official cult of Jupiter and his Olympian gods. His
successor, Marcus Aurelius, for all his enduring repute as a
great philosopher, writer, and ruler, was ruthless in his
treatment of Christians; many of the early fathers of the
church entered into martyrdom at the behest of the
philosopher-emperor whose bronze as, pictured here with
Neptune presiding over the royal galley, reveals his continued devotion to the gods of the old Roman religion.

Under Marcus Aurelius began the debasement of the
coinage which became so conspicuous in the Empire's later
years. Gradually the coins' content of precious metals was
reduced; often a supposedly silver piece was only a baser
metal thinly washed with silver. Some of the old coin denominations were being altered, too; within the ensuing

century or so the time-honored sestertius yielded its place as the portrait-piece of emperors to the double denarius, later called the follis.

The structure of Rome itself, like that of its coinage, was beginning to weaken. After Diocletian came to the throne in A.D. 284 the dissension and disunity within the empire were so pronounced that a scapegoat had to be found, and that scapegoat was, of course, the Christians. The ten-year period of violent persecution by Diocletian and his deputies and successors between A.D. 303 and 313 remains one of the darkest eras in all the annals of Christianity. (It is of interest to note, in passing, that the denarius which represents Diocletian here was struck at Londinium, now London, reminding us that Britannia was then still a Roman province.) This was the crowning struggle between the emperor who considered himself a god and the increasingly powerful group who refused to offer sacrifices in recognition of his divinity. Christians were condemned to death, their churches were demolished, their property was confiscated, they were denied all honors and employment, and in every possible way they were ruled to be outside the protection of the law and deprived of any redress for the measures invoked against them. Tortures and executions became commonplace.

Against such odds it would seem that Christianity should have been doomed, but it could no more be wiped out than could the Jewish religion be crushed by persecution of the Jews. A complicating factor was that, under Diocletian's very nose, many of the officials who were supposed to carry out his edicts had secretly become Christians themselves. Wherever the emperor cut off a head, two more seemed to spring up to take its place. It began to be apparent that the Roman people desired to be Christians, and when, after

some years of skirmishing for the succession, Constantine
the Great came into power, he was shrewd enough to bow
to the inevitable.

Even before Constantine attained undisputed sovereignty,
the Decree of Galerius, the Emperor of the East, in A.D. 311
gave Christianity legal recognition and granted to its followers equality with worshipers of the old gods. In view of
the fact that Galerius had been the most rabid of the
Christian-baiters, this was either a notable change of front
or else a frank admission that persecution was useless; but
Constantine went even further and transformed Christianity into the empire's official religion.

The stages by which he arrived at this decision never
have been entirely clear. Certainly he had no leanings
toward Christianity at the time of the striking of the follis
pictured here, showing him as a prince. Partly he was influenced to take this revolutionary step, no doubt, by
Helena, his mother, who was so ardent a Christian that she
made a long and taxing journey into Palestine and the
country of the Euphrates in her eagerness to find relics of
the life and crucifixion of Jesus. Significant of the honor in
which the emperor held her is the fact that in his very last
years, when at length he himself was about to embrace
Christianity, Constantine had his mother's portrait placed
upon the small bronze coin—a low-value coin of wide
common usage—which is reproduced here.

But to say that Helena won her son over to Christianity
is to close our eyes to the role which expediency must undoubtedly have played in Constantine's decision. The time
had come when Christianity was the religion not merely of
the slaves and the downtrodden but of many men of influence and standing. The struggle to suppress it was
seriously weakening the empire. Constantine, marveling at
the unifying force which the principles of Christianity

seemed to have upon its widely scattered and assorted followers, must have reasoned that if this great moral weapon were to be harnessed and encouraged, instead of being combated, it might be just what was needed to rally men's loyalty behind their empire and its leader. The cult of emperor worship was no longer adequate, but the power of the new religious faith might serve effectively to hold the empire together if the emperor himself were to give it his endorsement.

He chose a dramatic time and method for his pronouncement. Legend has it that just before his great victory at the battle of Milvian Bridge in A.D. 312 Constantine saw a cross flaming in the sky, accompanied by the words *In hoc signo vinces* (By this sign shalt thou conquer), and that the following night Christ appeared to him and told him to take the cross as the standard of his empire. [12] From this presumably supernatural background stems the symbolic use of the traditional Christian labarum—the first two letters of the Greek word for Christ superimposed upon each other—which Constantine used upon his shields and banners and, in particular, upon his coinage.

Whatever the merits of this miraculous legend, the fact remains that Constantine the Great not only encouraged Christianity from that time on but actively fostered its spread, and at length (though only after a curiously long delay) himself became a Christian. Except for a short lapse into opposition under Julian the Apostate, Christianity was now the specified religion of the empire—so much so, in fact, that eventually the worship of the old gods was forbidden and their lavish temples closed.

Less than a century after Constantine's passing the em-

[12] The first to preserve this familiar account of the turning point in Constantine's life was Eusebius of Caesarea, the fourth century church historian, in his *Historia Ecclesiastica*.

pire crumbled and perished, but the religion which it had
first fought and then accepted not only survived, but waxed
strong. To the imperial rulers of Rome Constantine's legendary *In hoc signo vinces* might no longer apply; but for the
Christians themselves it was so accurate a prophecy that
the reproduction here of that conquering sign, the labarum,
taken from a coin of one of Constantine's successors, makes
a fitting close to this narrative. Even in the realm of coinage,
which for centuries had glorified martial rulers and Greco-
Roman gods, veneration now was extended to the gentle,
unworldly teacher who had come to bring a new religion
of peace.

GLOSSARY

Ac' ti-um. Promontory at entrance to Ambracian Gulf on Ionian Sea in western Greece; scene of crucial naval victory of Octavius over Marc Antony, 31 B.C., by which he became emperor of Rome.

Ae-ge' an Sea. Arm of Mediterranean between Asia Minor and Greece.

Ae-gi' na (e-jī' na). Greek state on island nine miles long off southeastern coast of Greece.

Ae' li-a Cap-i-to-li' na (ē' li-a kap-i-to-lī' na). City built as Roman colony on ruins of Jerusalem by Emperor Hadrian, A.D. 135.

Aes-cu-la' pi-us. God of medicine and healing in Greek and Roman mythology, always shown holding a caduceus. (Greek form of name is usually *Asclepius*.)

A-grip' pa. See *Herod Agrippa*.

Ak' ra-gas (modern *Agrigento*). Commune in Sicily founded by Greek colonists in sixth century B.C.

Al-ex-an' der III (Alexander the Great), 356–323 B.C. King of Macedon and founder of short-lived Macedonian Empire.

Alexander IV, 323–310 B.C. Posthumous son of Alexander the Great, put to death by Cassander.

Alexander Jan-nae' us. See *Maccabees*.

Al-ex-an' dri-a. Large commercial city and seaport of Egypt founded by Alexander the Great.

Alexandria Tro' as. Seaport of Mysia, south of site of ancient Troy; visited by Paul on second and third journeys.

al-loy' . A mixture of two or more metals.

Al-y-at' tes. King of Lydia 617–560 B.C.; pioneer in coinage; father of Croesus.

Am' mon. Sun god of ancient Egyptians.

Am-phip' o-lis. Ancient city of eastern Macedonia.

AM' PHO-RA. Tall two-handled earthenware jar for wine or oil.

AN-A-NI' AS. Chief of the council of priests before whom Paul was brought for judgment in Jerusalem, A.D. 53.

AN' NAS. High priest at Jerusalem before whom Jesus, and later Peter and John, were brought; father-in-law of *Caiaphas*.

AN-TIG' O-NUS II. Last Maccabean ruler of Judea; king 40–37 B.C.

AN' TI-OCH. City on the Orontes near the Mediterranean, founded by Seleucus I; capital of Syria before Roman conquest; mission center for early Christianity.

AN-TI' O-CHUS I, called ANTIOCHUS SO' TER. King of Syria 280–261 B.C

ANTIOCHUS II, called ANTIOCHUS THEOS. King of Syria 261–247 B.C.

ANTIOCHUS III, called ANTIOCHUS THE GREAT. King of Syria 223–187 B.C.

ANTIOCHUS IV, called ANTIOCHUS E-PIPH' A-NES. King of Syria 175–163 B.C.; oppressor of Jews who brought on Wars of the Maccabees and lost Jerusalem.

ANTIOCHUS VII, called ANTIOCHUS SI-DE' TES. King of Syria 138–129 B.C.; besieger of Jerusalem in 133 B.C.

AN-TIP' A-TER, 398?–319 B.C. Regent of Macedonia during Alexander III's eleven years' absence and after Alexander's death.

ANTIPATER THE ID-U-MAE' AN. Procurator of Judea 47–43 B.C.; father of Herod the Great.

AN-TO-NI' NUS PI' US (Ti' tus Au-re' li-us Ful' vius Boi-o' ni-us Ar' ri-us), A.D. 86–161. Emperor of Rome, 138–161.

AN' TO-NY, MARC, 83–30 B.C. Roman general; member of triumvirate ruling Rome after assassination of Caesar.

APH-RO-DI' TE. Greek goddess of love and beauty, identified with Roman Venus.

A-POC' RY-PHA. Books of Jewish religious history not in canonical Hebrew Scriptures and not included in most Protestant Bibles.

A-POL' LO. Greek and Roman sun god; god of youth, music, prophecy, and manly beauty.

A-QUIL' A AND PRIS-CIL' LA. Jewish tentmakers with whom Paul lodged at Corinth. Driven from Rome A.D. 49 by edict of Claudius, they became Christian converts.

AR' A-DUS (now *Arwad*). Island seaport of ancient Phoenicia.

AR-CHE-LA' US (ar-ke-lā' us). See *Herod Archelaus*.

AR' E-TAS. Name of several kings of Nabataean Arabs of northwestern Arabia.

A-RIS-TO-BU' LUS. See *Maccabees*.

AR-SIN' O-Ë I. Daughter of Lysimachus of Thrace and first wife of Ptolemy II of Egypt, who banished her to marry his sister.

ARSINOË II. Daughter of Ptolemy I and Berenice I of Egypt; in 276 B.C. became second wife of her brother, Ptolemy II.

AR' TE-MIS. See *Diana*.

AS. Roman bronze coin, of varying size and value, worth roughly about a cent. Also known as "third bronze."

AS-CLE' PI-US. See *Aesculapius*.

AS-PEN' dus. City of ancient Pamphylia in Asia Minor.

AS-SA' RI-ON. Small Greek bronze coin of low value.

AS-SYR' I-A (known also as AS' SHUR). Ancient empire of western Asia, at its height from 12th to 7th centuries B.C.; conquered Israel 734 B.C.

A-THE' NA. Greek goddess of wisdom and patroness of the arts, identified with Roman *Minerva*. Patron goddess of Athens.

ATH' ENS. Leading city-state of ancient Greece.

AT' TIC. Pertaining to Attica, the district of Greece of which Athens was the principal city.

AU-GUS' TUS (Ga' ius Jul' ius Cae' sar Oc-ta-vi-a' nus). 63 B.C.–A.D. 14. First Roman emperor, 27 B.C.–A.D. 14.

AUGUSTUS. Distinctive title reserved for use of a reigning Roman emperor.

AU-RE' LI-US, MAR' CUS. See *Marcus Aurelius*.

BA' AL (bā' al). The sun-god, worshiped in Canaan, Phoenicia, Syria, and other ancient Arabic nations.

BAB' Y-LON. Ancient empire of Euphrates Valley in southwestern Asia; reached greatest heights in 20th and in 6th centuries B.C.

BA-NI' YAS. See *Caesarea Philippi*.

BAR CO' CHE-BA (ko' ke-va), SI' MON. Leader of Second Jewish Revolt against Rome, A.D. 132–135, at end of which he was slain.

BEL-LER' O-PHON. Mythological Greek hero who perished in attempt to reach heaven on winged horse Pegasus.

BEL-LO' NA. In Roman mythology the goddess of war.

BEL-SHAZ' ZAR. King of Babylon when it was conquered by Cyrus in 539 B.C.

BER-E-NI' CE I (ber-e-nī' se). Wife and half-sister of Ptolemy I of Egypt.

BI' GA. Two-horse chariot.

BOE-O' TIA (be-ō' sha).   Ancient republic in east central Greece.

BOE-O' TIAN LEAGUE.   Federation of city-states of eastern central
 Greece under leadership of Thebes in sixth to third centuries B.C.

BRASS.   An alloy of copper and zinc.

BRONZE.   An alloy of copper and tin.

BUL' LION.   Uncoined gold or silver in mass.

CA.   Generally interpreted as abbreviation for *Commune of Asia* in
 the Roman Empire.

CA-BI' RI (ku-bī' rī).   Beneficent deities of early Greek religion, perhaps of Phoenician origin; patrons of navigation and of metal
 workers. They were worshiped in secret.

CA-DU' CE-US.   Staff on which two serpents twine, used as emblem of
 Greco-Roman god of medicine, Aesculapius. Also an attribute of
 Hermes, messenger of the gods.

CAE' SAR.   Generic title for any Roman emperor. Specifically, the
 title (roughly synonymous with "Prince") given a young man upon
 association with the emperor in government.

CAE-SA-RE' A.   Roman capital of Palestine; seaport on coast of
 Samaria 55 miles northwest of Jerusalem.

CAESAREA PHI-LIP' PI.   Ancient city at foot of Mount Hermon near
 source of Jordan in northwestern Palestine. Named for Philip the
 Tetrarch, who rebuilt it. Called *Paneas* in pre-Roman times. (Modern *Baniyas* in southwestern Syria.)

CA' IA-PHAS (kā' ya-fas), JOSEPH.   High priest at Jerusalem from
 about A.D. 18 to 36; presiding officer at trial which condemned
 Jesus to death.

CA-LIG' ULA (Ga' ius Caésar), A.D. 12–41.   Roman emperor 37–41;
 insane.

CA' NAAN.   Old name of that part of Palestine between Jordan and
 Mediterranean.

CA-PER' NA-UM.   City of ancient Palestine on northwestern shore of
 Sea of Galilee; home of Jesus during most of period of his ministry.

CAS-SAN' DER.   King of Macedon 316–297 B.C.

CAS' TOR AND POL' LUX.   In Roman mythology twin sons of Jupiter
 and Leda.

CA-TA' NI-A.   Town in eastern Sicily at foot of Mount Etna.

CEN' SOR.   A Roman magistrate; term often used in connection with
 emperor's titles to show ruler was Rome's chief magistrate.

CHAL' CUS (kal' cus).   Small Greek copper coin.

CHA-SI′ DIM (ka-sē′ dim). Literally "the pious"; zealous adherents of rigid Judaism, 300–175 B.C., who led resistance to Antiochus IV's decrees violating Mosaic laws.

CHI′ OS (ki′ os). Island in Aegean Sea west of Ephesus and Smyrna, visited several times by Paul; reputed birthplace of Homer.

CI-LI′ CI-A (si-lish′ a). Ancient country on Mediterranean coast in southeastern Asia Minor; was made a Roman province by Pompey the Great.

CLAU′ DI-US I (Ti-be′ ri-us Clau′ di-us Dru′ sus Ne′ ro Ger-man′ i-cus), 10 B.C.–A.D. 54, Roman emperor 41–54.

CLE-O-PA′ TRA I. Daughter of Antiochus III of Syria and wife of Ptolemy V of Egypt.

CON′ STAN-TINE I (CONSTANTINE THE GREAT), A.D. 280?–337. Roman emperor 306–337; convert to Christianity; founder of Constantinople as new capital of Roman Empire.

CON′ SUL. One of the two chief magistrates of the Roman state.

COP′ PER. Term used loosely to describe coins of uncertain alloy; roughly synonymous with *bronze*.

COR′ INTH. City and seaport of northeastern Peloponnesus in southern Greece.

COUN′ TER-MARK. A secondary stamp placed on an old coin, usually either for revaluation purposes or to give the coin a fresh guarantee by a new authority.

CROE′ SUS (krē′ sus). Last king of Lydia, during whose reign (560–546 B.C.) important developments in coinage occurred.

CYB′ E-LE. In classical mythology the mother of the gods; called also *Rhe′ a*.

CY′ RUS. King of Persia 550–529 B.C.; founder of Persian Empire; deliverer of Jews from captivity in Babylon.

DA-MAS′ CUS. Ancient commercial city of Syria, ruled in turn by Egyptians, Hittites, Assyrians, Babylonians, Persians, Greeks, Ptolemies, Seleucids, and Romans.

DAR′ IC. Ancient Persian gold coin weighing about 129 grains and worth about $5.50.

DA-RI′ US I (DARIUS THE GREAT). King of Persia 521–486 B.C.

DARIUS THE MEDE. Conqueror of Babylon and successor to Belshazzar on throne, according to Bible but not according to recorded secular history.

DE-BASE′ MENT. Reduction of coinage's purity, quality, or value.

DE-ME' TRI-US.   Silversmith of Ephesus, first century A.D., who organized opposition to Paul's Christian teachings.

DE-NA' RI-US.   Roman silver coin worth at first ten and later sixteen asses, roughly about 15.5 cents in U.S. money. Translated as "penny" in King James Version.

DI-AN' A.   Moon goddess of Roman mythology, worshiped as patroness of human fertility. (The Greek *Artemis.*)

DI' DRACHM (dī' dram).   Greek silver coin worth two drachmas (18 to 38 cents).

DI-LEP' TON.   Copper coin worth two lepta (about .4 cent).

DI-O-CLE' TIAN   (Ga' ius Au-re' li-us Va-le' ri-us Di-o-cle-ti-a' nus), A.D. 245–313.   Roman emperor 284–305; extreme persecutor of Christians.

DI-O-NY' SOS.   Greek god of wine and drama, identified with Roman *Bacchus.*

DI-OS-CU' RI.   See *Castor and Pollux.*

DI-O' TA.   Wine jug.

DO-MI' TIAN (Ti' tus Fla' vi-us Do-mi-ti-a' nus Au-gus' tus), A.D. 51–96.   Third and last Flavian emperor of Rome, 81–96.

DOUBLE DE-NA' RI-US.   Bronze Roman coin first issued in late third century A.D. Usually called *follis.*

DRACHM (dram).   Same as *drachma.*

DRACH' MA (drak' ma).   Greek silver coin of varying weights, worth from 9 to 19 cents in current terms. (In fifth century B.C. it was a day's pay for a first-class workman.)

DRAM.   Same as *drachma.*

DU-PON' DI-US.   Rome's "second bronze" coin, worth one-eighth of a denarius or approximately two cents. Also known as "medium bronze."

DYR-RHA' CHI-UM.   Seaport on eastern coast of the Adriatic founded by Greek colonists in 7th century B.C. (Modern *Durrës* in Albania.)

EL-E-A'-ZAR.   Son of Ananias; captain of the temple at Jerusalem who led Jews at outset of First Revolt against Rome in A.D. 66.

E-LEC' TRUM.   A natural alloy of gold and silver.

E' LIS.   Ancient country and city of Peloponnesus in southern Greece; scene of Olympian games.

EPH' E-SUS.   Ionian city of western Asia Minor near Aegean Sea. Center of cult of Diana and site of temple of Diana of Ephesus. Early seat of Christianity.

E' PHRON (ē' fron). Hittite who sold Cave of Machpelah to Abraham.

E-PIPH' A-NES. See *Antiochus IV.*

ETH' ROG. Fruit of citron tree, used in ancient Jewish religious ceremonies.

ET' NA, MOUNT. Volcano in eastern Sicily.

EU-PHRA' TES. River flowing 1,700 miles through Mesopotamia and Babylonia to unite with Tigris and empty into Persian Gulf.

EX-ERGUE' (egz-erg'). The space below principal design on coin's reverse. In Roman times it was often inscribed with name of city where coin was minted.

FAR' THING. British coin worth about half a cent in U.S. money. Term applied to small New Testament coins by translators of King James Version of Bible.

FE' LIX, AN-TO' NI-US. Greek freedman of Emperor Claudius; procurator of Judea (*c.* A.D. 52–60) under whom Paul was tried and kept prisoner.

FES' TUS, POR' -CI-US (por' shus). Roman procurator of Judea (*c.* A.D. 60–62) before whom Paul made his "appeal unto Caesar."

FIELD. Portion of coin not covered by design.

FIRST BRONZE. See *sestertius.*

FIRST REVOLT. Insurrection of Jews against Roman rule, A.D. 66–70.

FLAN. The metal blank on which coin types are struck.

FLA' VI-US. Name of a Roman clan or family, three of whose members—Vespasian and his sons Titus and Domitian—became emperors of Rome known as the Flavians.

FLO' RUS, GES' SI-US (jesh' us). Procurator of Judea under Nero at outbreak of First Revolt of Jews.

FOL' LIS. Large bronze coin introduced by Diocletian in his reform of Roman coinage in late third century A.D.

FOR-TU' NA. Roman goddess of fortune or chance, analogous to Greek *Tyche.*

GAL' BA, SER' VI-US SUL-PI' CI-US (5? B.C.–A.D. 69). Roman emperor for six months, 68–69.

GA-LE' RI-US (Ga' ius Ga-lé ri-us Va-lé ri-us Max-im-i-a' nus). Roman emperor of the East, A.D. 305–311; severe persecutor of Christians.

GAL' LUS, GA' IUS CES' tius. Roman governor of Syria in the time of Nero.

GE-HA' ZI. Servant of Elisha.

GER' I-ZIM, MOUNT.   Peak of 2,849 feet just south of Shechem (later Neapolis and now Nablus) in Samaria, Palestine; sacred place of worship for Samaritans.

GRA' TUS, VA-LE' RI-US.   Procurator of Judea under Tiberius, immediately preceding Pontius Pilate.

HA' DRI-AN (Pub' li-us Ae' li-us Ha-dri-a' nus), A.D. 76–138.   Roman emperor during whose reign (117–138) occurred Second Revolt of Jews.

HA-RAN'.   Ancient city of northern Mesopotamia; residence of Abraham before his migration to Canaan.

HAS-MO-NAE' AN.   Family name of the *Maccabees*.

HEL' E-NA.   Mother of Constantine the Great, who became a Christian saint in recognition of her devotion to Christian cause, her pilgrimage to Jerusalem (about A.D. 325), and her construction of Christian churches there.

HEL-LEN' IC.   Grecian.

HER' A-KLES.   Hero representing strength and endurance in Greek mythology; equivalent to Roman *Hercules*.

HER' CU-LES.   Roman name for *Herakles*.

HER' MES.   Herald and messenger of the gods in Greek mythology; identified with Roman *Mercury*.

HER' MON, MOUNT.   Mountain near source of river Jordan in northwestern Palestine.

HER' OD.   Name of dynasty ruling Palestine in first centuries B.C. and A.D.

HEROD A-GRIP' PA I.   King of Judea A.D. 41–44.   Caused death of Apostle James and imprisonment of Peter.

HEROD AGRIPPA II, A.D. 27?–100.   Puppet king of Judea at time of Paul's imprisonment and First Revolt of Jews.

HEROD AR-CHE-LA' US (ar-ke-la' us).   Son of Herod the Great; ruler over Judea and Samaria 4 B.C.–A.D. 6 at time of return from Egypt of Joseph, Mary, and Jesus.

HEROD THE GREAT, 73?–4 B.C.   King of Judea at time of birth of Jesus.

HE-RO' DI-AS.   Sister of Herod Agrippa I; wife of Herod Philip and Herod Antipas; mother of Salome.

HO-MER' IC.   Period of ancient Greece described in *Iliad* and *Odyssey*.

HYR-CA' NUS.   See *Maccabees*.

ID-U-ME' A.   Country of the Edomites in southern Palestine.

IM-PE-RA′ TOR. Title bestowed on victorious military commanders under Roman Republic and very early Empire; later an official designation reserved to emperor alone.

IN-CUSE′. Impression, usually square, made by a reverse die or moneyer's punch. Term is also used to describe a reverse which is an intaglio impression of obverse.

IN′ GOT. A mass of unworked metal.

I-RAN′. See *Persia*.

I′ SIS. Egyptian goddess of arts, agriculture, and fertility.

JAD′ DU-A. High priest who staved off destruction of Jerusalem by Alexander the Great in 334 B.C.

JAN-NAE′ US. See *Maccabees*.

JA′ NUS. Roman deity having two faces; god of past and future.

JE-RU′ SA-LEM. Capital of kingdom of Israel and later of Judea.

JO-SE′ PHUS, FLAVIUS, A.D. 37?–100. Jewish historian and general; participant in First Revolt of the Jews; protégé of Emperors Vespasian, Titus, and Domitian; author of *History of the Jewish Wars* and *Antiquities of the Jews*.

JU′ DA-ISM. Jewish beliefs and practices.

JU-DE′ A. Southern division of Palestine under Persian, Greek, Egyptian, Syrian, Roman, and sometimes independent rule.

JU′ LIAN THE A-POS′ TATE (Fla′ vi-us Clau′ di-us Ju-li-a′ nus), A.D. 331–363. Roman emperor 361–363; convert to paganism and enemy of Christianity.

JU′ PI-TER. Supreme god of the Romans; identified with Greek Zeus.

LAB′ A-RUM. Greek monogram of Christ adopted by Constantine the Great as insignia for Roman coins and for military and ecclesiastical standards.

LA-OD′ I-CE. Wife of Antiochus II of Syria.

LA-OD-I-CE′ A. City in Phrygia, west central Asia Minor, founded in third century B.C. by Antiochus II of Seleucid Dynasty; later an early center of Christian missions.

"LARGE MONEY." Term used in Roman times to distinguish large silver coins, such as tetradrachms, from small ones, such as denarii.

LA′ TI-UM. Ancient country of west central Italy inhabited by Latins; dominated by Rome from 5th century B.C.

LEG′ END. Lettering inscribed on coin.

LEP′ TON. Small Greek copper coin, worth possibly 1/6 of a cent; translated as "mite" in New Testament.

LIV' I-A DRU-SIL' LA, 56? B.C.–A.D. 29.   First Roman empress; third
wife of Octavius, who became Emperor Augustus; mother of
Tiberius.

LON-DIN' -I-UM.   Roman name for London.

LU' LAB.   Bundle of palm and willow branches carried by Jews at
Feast of Tabernacles.

LYD' I-A.   Ancient country of western Asia Minor. According to
Herodotus and tradition it was the birthplace of coinage.

LY-SIM' A-CHUS, 361?–281 B.C.   Macedonian general who received
rule over Thrace after death of Alexander the Great; later became
king.

MAC' CA-BEES.   Jewish patriots of *Hasmonaean* family, second and first
centuries B.C. Leaders included MAT-TA-THI' AS, father and
founder; his sons JU' DAS (leader 166–160 B.C.), JON' A-THAN (leader
160–143 B.C.), and SI' MON (143–134 B.C.); Simon's son JOHN HYR-
CA' NUS (leader 134–104 B.C.); John Hyrcanus' sons A-RIS-TO-
BU' LUS I (104–103 B.C.) and ALEXANDER JAN-NAE' US (103–76
B.C.); SA-LO' ME ALEXANDRA, wife of Alexander Jannaeus (76–67
B.C.); her sons HYRCANUS II and ARISTOBULUS II, who warred for
throne until Roman conquest, 63 B.C.; the latter's son AN-TIG' O-
NUS II (40–37 B.C.); and Antigonus II's niece MAR-I-AM' NE, second
wife of *Herod the Great.*

MAC' E-DON.   Kingdom on central Balkan Peninsula which achieved
rule over Greece and other countries under Philip II and Alexander the Great.

MACH-PE' LAH.   Cave near town of Hebron in central Palestine,
where the Bible says Abraham and Sarah and their children were
buried.

MAG' IS-TRATE.   In numismatic usage: mint official responsible for
supervision of coinage.

MAG-NEN' TIUS (mag-nen' shus), FLA' VI-US PO-PIL' I-US.   Roman
emperor of the West, A.D. 350–353.

MAR' A-THON.   Plain 24 miles northeast of Athens on which outnumbered Greek army defeated Persian invaders in 490 B.C.

MAR' A-THON.   Footrace of 26 miles 385 yards, commemorating legendary run of messenger who brought news to Athens of victory
at Marathon.

MARC AN'TO-NY.   See *Antony, Marc.*

MAR' CUS AU-RE' LI-US (Marcus An' ni-us Aurelius Ve' rus), A.D. 121–180. Emperor of Rome 161–180.

MAR-I-AM' NE THE HAS-MO-NAE' AN, 60?–29 B.C. Granddaughter of the Maccabean ruler Hyrcanus II; second wife of Herod the Great (who executed her); grandmother of Herod Agrippa II.

MAT-TA-THI' AS. See *Maccabees.*

ME' DI-A. Ancient country of southern Asia (northwestern part of modern Iran); became province of Persia before conquest by Alexander the Great.

MEL' KARTH or MEL' KART. Principal deity of ancient Tyre, i.e., the local designation for *Baal.*

MER' CU-RY. Herald and messenger of gods in Roman mythology; identified with Greek *Hermes.*

MES-O-PO-TA' MI-A. Region in southwestern Asia between Tigris and Euphrates rivers.

MET-A-PON' TUM. City in southern Italy founded by Greek colonists about 700 B.C.

MID' I-AN-ITES. Traditional enemies of Israelites in Old Testament times; residents of northwestern Arabia.

MIL' VI-AN BRIDGE. Bridge across Tiber just north of Rome near scene of Emperor Constantine's victory over Maxentius in A.D. 312.

MI' NA (mī' na). Weight of Old Testament period, valued at 50 shekels. (Greek mina equaled 100 drachmas.)

MI-NER' VA. Roman goddess of wisdom, identified with Greek *Athena.*

MINT. Place for legal manufacture and issue of coins.

MITE. See *lepton.*

MO' DIN. Town in Judea about 15 miles northwest of Jerusalem, where Mattathias, founder of Maccabee family, was priest at time of invasion by Antiochus Epiphanes.

MON' EY-ER. An authorized coiner of money.

NA' A-MAN (nā' a-man). Syrian captain cured of leprosy by Elisha.

NA-BA-TE' A. Region in northwestern Arabia.

NA' HOR (nā' hor). Brother of Abraham and grandfather of Rebekah.

NE-AP' O-LIS. See *Shechem.*

NEB-U-CHAD-NEZ' ZAR. King of Babylon 605–562 B.C.; conqueror of Palestine and Jerusalem.

NE' ME-A.   Valley in northeastern part of Peloponnesus in ancient
Greece; in Greek mythology the scene of Herakles's slaying of
Nemean lion.

NEP' TUNE.   God of the sea in Roman mythology.

NE' RO (Ne' ro Clau' di-us Cae' sar Dru' sus Brit-tan' i-cus), A.D.
37–68.   Roman emperor, 54–68.

NER' VA, MAR' CUS COC-CE' IUS (kok-se' yus), A.D. 35?–98.   Roman
emperor 96–98.

NI'KE (ni' kee).   Goddess of victory in Greek mythology. Similar to
Roman *Victoria* or *Winged Victory.*

NU-MIS-MAT' ICS.   The science of coins and medals, derived from
Greek word for coins.

OB' VERSE.   The face of a coin.

OC-TA' VI-US, GA' IUS.   See *Augustus.*

O-LYM' PI-A.   Plain in northwestern Peloponnesus of ancient Greece;
scene of Olympian Games.

O-LYM' PI-AS.   Mother of Alexander the Great; killed by Cassander
in 316 B.C.

O-LYM' PUS.   Mountain range in northeastern Greece; home of the
gods of Greek mythology.

O' THO, MAR' CUS SAL' VI-US, A.D. 32–69.   Roman emperor for three
months in 69.

O' VER-STRIKE.   To strike an old coin with a new type or design after
obliterating or partially obliterating the old one by hammering or
melting.

PAL' A-TINE.   One of the seven hills of Rome.

PAM-PHYL' I-A.   Ancient district on northern Mediterranean coast
in southern Asia Minor, subject in turn to many empires.

PA-NE' AS.   See *Caesarea Philippi.*

PA' PHOS.   Town and district on southwestern coast of island of
Cyprus, ruled in turn by Phoenicians, Greeks, Ptolemies, and
Romans; visited by Paul.

PAR' THI-A.   Ancient country in western Asia (now northeastern
Iran), known at its height as Parthian Empire.

PA' TER PA' TRI-AE.   "Father of his country"—a title bestowed on
various Roman emperors by the Senate.

PAT' MOS.   One of the Dodecanese islands in southeastern Aegean
Sea; scene of St. John's exile.

PAX.   Feminine figure personifying *Peace* on Roman coins.

PE-CU′ NI-A. Roman word for *money*, derived from the Latin word *pecus*, for cattle.

PEG′ A-SUS. Winged horse of Greek mythology.

PEL-O-PON-NE′ SUS. Peninsula forming southern part of mainland of Greece.

"PENNY." Translation of Roman coin *denarius* (worth over 15 cents) in King James Version of the Bible. The English penny was originally a silver coin equivalent to the denarius.

PER′ GA. Chief town of Pamphylia, where Paul and Barnabas began their first mission in Asia Minor.

PER′ GA-MOS. City in ancient Mysia, Asia Minor; for a time capital of the Roman province of Asia; early seat of Christianity.

PER-SEP′ O-LIS. Ancient capital of Persia, founded by Darius the Great.

PER′ SIA (I-RAN′). Ancient empire of southwestern Asia, reaching its height from 6th to 4th centuries B.C.

PHAR′ I-SEES. Members of exclusive ancient Jewish sect which paid extreme regard to tradition and ceremonies.

PHIL-A-DEL′ PHUS. See *Ptolemy II.*

PHIL′ IP II (PHILIP of MACEDON), 382–336 B.C. King of Macedon, 359–336; conqueror of Greece; father of Alexander the Great.

PHILIP THE TE′ TRARCH. Son of Herod the Great; husband of Salome; ruler of northern section of Palestine, 4 B.C.–A.D. 34. Sometimes called Herod Philip II.

PHOE-NI′ CI-A. Ancient maritime country in western Syria bordering the Mediterranean.

PI′ LATE, PON′ TIUS (pon′ shus). Procurator of Judea under Tiberius after A.D. 26; delivered Jesus to be crucified.

PLANCH′ ET. Same as *flan.*

POL′ LUX. See *Castor.*

POM′ PEY THE GREAT (GNAE′ US POM-PE′ IUS MAG′ NUS), 106–48 B.C. Roman general and statesman; rival of Caesar; conqueror of Palestine.

PON′ TI-FEX MAX′ I-MUS. Literally "head priest"; title held by each Roman emperor as head of Roman religion.

PRIS-CIL′ LA. See *Aquila.*

PROC′ U-RA-TOR. A Roman governor or provincial administrator.

PTOL′ E-MY (tŏl′ ĕ-mĭ). Name of many kings of Egypt from 323 to 30 B.C., comprising the Ptolemaic Dynasty.

PTOLEMY I, called PTOLEMY SO' TER.   King of Egypt 323–285 B.C.

PTOLEMY II, called PTOLEMY PHIL-A-DEL' PHUS.   King of Egypt 285–246 B.C.

PTOLEMY III, called PTOLEMY EU-ER' GE-TES.   King of Egypt 246–221 B.C.

PTOLEMY V, called PTOLEMY E-PIPH' A-NES.   King of Egypt 203–181 B.C.

PTOLEMY VI, called PTOLEMY PHIL-O-ME' TOR.   King of Egypt 181–145 B.C.

PUNCH.   Metal tool with design projecting from its face, used to make impression on face of die or (in very ancient days) of coin itself.

PU' NIC WARS.   Rome's three wars with Carthage: 264–241, 218–201, and 149–146 B.C.

QUAD' RANS.   Roman copper coin worth one-fourth of an as.

QUAD-RI' GA.   Two-wheeled racing chariot drawn by four horses harnessed abreast.

QUI-NA' RI-US.   Roman silver coin of one-half-denarius value (about eight cents).

RE-STRIKE'.   Same as *overstrike*.

RE-VERSE' .   The back or secondary side of a coin.

RO' MA.   Goddess personifying Rome.

RO-SET' TA STONE.   Table bearing inscriptions in Greek and in two forms of Egyptian hieroglyphics which provided key to ancient Egyptian inscriptions.

ROX-AN' A.   Wife of Alexander the Great. Put to death by Cassander, 310 B.C.

SAD' DU-CEES.   Members of skeptical Jewish sect, originating in second century B.C., whose members adhered only to Mosaic law.

SA-LO' ME, *c.* A.D. 14–62.   Daughter of Herodias and Herod Philip; granddaughter of Herod the Great; wife of Philip the Tetrarch.

SALOME AL-EX-AN' DRA.   See *Maccabees*.

SA-MAR' I-A.   District of ancient Palestine extending from Mediterranean to Jordan south of Galilee and north of Judea.

SANDAN.   Oriental god corresponding roughly to Greek Herakles.

SAR' DIS.   Principal city of ancient Lydia; possible site of mint where earliest known coinage was struck.

SC.   Inscription on Roman bronze coins meaning *Senatus Consulto* (with the consent of the Senate).

SCAU' RUS, MAR' CUS AE-MI' LIUS.   Quaestor (treasurer) to Pompey the Great at time of first Roman conquest of Jerusalem.

SECOND BRONZE. See *dupondius*.

SECOND REVOLT. Insurrection of Jews against Roman rule, A.D. 132–135.

SE-CU' RI-TAS. Feminine figure personifying Confidence or Security on Roman coins.

SE-LEU' CI-A. (se-lu' shi-a). City on west bank of Tigris founded by Seleucus I in 312 B.C. as chief city of Seleucid Empire.

SE-LEU' CI-DAE. A dynasty (312–64 B.C.) which at its height ruled over Bactria, Persia, Babylonia, Syria, and part of Asia Minor.

SE-LEU' CUS I, 358?–280 B.C. Macedonian general under Alexander the Great; founder of Seleucid dynasty.

SE' MIS. Roman bronze coin of half-as value.

SEN-NACH' ER-IB (sĕ-năk' cr-ib). King of Assyria, 705–681 B.C., who invaded Palestine and besieged Jerusalem.

SES-TER' TI-US (ses-ter' shi-us). Roman coin, originally of silver and worth a quarter of a denarius, i.e., about four cents. During the empire it was of bronze. (Also called "first bronze" and "large bronze.")

SEX' TANS. Bronze coin of early Roman Republic valued at one-sixth of an as.

SHE' CHEM (shē' kem). Name in Biblical times of town in Samaria 30 miles north of Jerusalem between Mount Ebal and Mount Gerizim. Also called *Sychar* in Bible. Rebuilt and renamed *Neapolis* by Emperor Vespasian. Now called *Nablus*.

SHEK' EL (shĕk' el).
1. Hebrew, Assyrian, and Babylonian unit of weight, probably about 1 1/3 or 1 1/2 ounces.
2. Silver coin used by Judea and near-by nations; value approximately same as that of tetradrachm (about 60 to 76 cents).

SHEW' BREAD. Loaves of unleavened bread set forth in sanctuary in Jewish ritual.

SI-DE' TES. See *Antiochus VII*.

SI' DON (modern *Sa-i' da*). A powerful city-state and in early times a chief city of Phoenicia.

SIG' LOS (pl. SIGLOI). Persian silver coin weighing about 80 grains; value 1/20 that of Persian gold daric, i.e., about 27 cents.

SI' MON. Name used on Judean coins to represent *Simon Bar Cocheba*, leader of Second Revolt of Jews.

SPAR' TA. Ancient city of southern Greece; leader of Peloponnesian League.

SPE' CIE (spē' shie). Coined money.

SPES.   Feminine figure personifying Hope on Roman coins.

STAMP.   To make marks or pattern on coin blank by impressing it with a die.

STAT' ER.

1. Principal gold coin of ancient Greece. Of varying value, but usually about $5.50.

2. Any standard principal coin, either gold or silver, of Greece or other Mediterranean nations.

STRIKE.   To impress a device on one or both sides of a coin blank.

SU' SA.   Ancient city of Elam at head of Persian Gulf; one of the capitals of Persian Empire under Cyrus the Great.

SY' CHAR (sȳ' kar).   See *Shechem.*

SYR' A-CUSE.   Important seaport city of southeastern Sicily.

SYR' I-A.   Ancient country at east end of Mediterranean Sea, in turn part of Egyptian, Babylonian, Assyrian, Persian, and Roman empires; independent under Seleucid dynasty.

TAL' ENT.   Ancient Hebrew weight equivalent to 3,000 shekels, 60 minae, or nearly 94 pounds avoirdupois. (Attic talent was about 57 pounds.) Estimates of its monetary value in gold and silver vary widely.

TAR' SUS.   Chief city of Silicia. Birthplace of Paul.

TET' RA-DRACHM (tet' ra-dram).   Greek silver coin worth four drachmas, or 36 to 76 cents (more often given as the latter). International monetary standard of ancient world.

THA' SOS.   Greek island in northern Aegean Sea off Macedonia and Thrace.

THEBES.   Old city of eastern central Greece 33 miles northwest of Athens; head of Boeotian League.

THE' OS.   Greek word for god.

THES-SA-LO-NI' CA.

1. Half-sister of Alexander the Great, wife of Cassander.

2. Seaport city of west central Macedonia in northeastern Greece, named in her honor.

THIRD BRONZE.   See *as.*

THRACE.   Ancient kingdom bordering northeastern Aegean Sea.

TI' BER.   River which flows through Rome.

TI-BE' -RI-US CLAU' DI-US NE' RO, 42 B.C.–A.D. 37.   Second emperor of Rome, A.D. 14–37.

TI' TUS FLA' VI-US SA-BI' NUS VES-PA-SI-A' NUS, 40?–A.D. 81.   Conqueror of Jerusalem A.D. 70. Rome's second Flavian emperor, 79–81.

TRIB' UNE. Originally a representative chosen by Rome's plebeians to protect them against patrician oppression; later a title used by emperor as supreme civil head of the state.

"TRIBUTE PENNY." Denarius of Emperor Tiberius.

TRI' DRACHM (trī' dram). Greek silver coin worth three drachmas (27 to 57 cents).

TRI' ENS. Bronze coin of early Roman Republic, equal to one-third of an as.

TY' che (tȳ' kē). Greek goddess of luck or fortune.

TYPE. Design on coin.

TYRE. Powerful maritime and commercial city of antiquity on eastern Mediterranean coast; capital of ancient Phoenicia.

UN' CI-A. Bronze coin of early Roman Republic, valued at one-twelfth of an as.

UR OF THE CHAL-DEES' (kăl-dēz). City and district in southern part of ancient Babylonia on a former channel of Euphrates River; birthplace of Abraham.

VA-LE' RI-US GRA' TUS. Procurator of Judea under Emperor Tiberius, serving just before Pontius Pilate.

VES-PA' SIAN (Ti' tus FLA' vi-us Sa-bi' nus Ves-pa-si-a' nus), A.D. 9–79. General in command of Roman troops against Jews in First Revolt; first Flavian emperor of Rome, 69–79.

VIC-TO' RI-A. Female figure, sometimes winged, personifying victory on Roman coins; similar to Greek *Nike*.

VI-TEL' LI-US, AU' LUS, A.D. 15–69. Roman emperor eleven months in 69.

WINGED VICTORY. See *Victoria*.

ZE-RUB' BA-BEL. Governor of Jerusalem who led returning exiles from Babylon about 538 B.C.

ZEUS. Father of the gods in Greek mythology; identified with Roman Jupiter.

ZI' ON. Height in Jerusalem; site of temple and other important buildings which made it center of Jewish national life and hence synonym for Jerusalem.

Appendix 2

BIBLIOGRAPHY

Adams, Sebastian C., *Syn-chronological Chart or Map of History*. Chicago, Andrews, 1871. Illustrated.

Akerman, John Yonge, *Numismatic Illustrations of the Narrative Portions of the New Testament*. London, Smith, 1846. 62 pp.; 31 woodcuts.

Angus, Joseph, and F. S. Hoyt, *The Bible Hand-book*. Philadelphia, Fagan, 1883. 788–xx pp.; maps, portraits, and 300 illustrations.

Breasted, J. H., *The Conquest of Civilization*. New York, Harper, 1938. 669 pp.; illustrated.

Catalogue of Greek Coins in the British Museum, A. 29 vols. London, British Museum, 1883–1927. Illustrated.

Clarke, Adam, *Clarke's Commentary*. New York, Carlton & Porter, 1817. 6 vols.

Cohen, Henry, *Description historique des monnaies frappées sous l'empire romain*, 2nd ed. Paris, Rollin, 1880.

Durant, Will, *The Life of Greece*. New York, Simon & Schuster, 1939. 755 pp.; illustrated.

Encyclopaedia Britannica, 11th ed., Vol. XIX, pp. 893–895 on Roman coins.

Fallows, Samuel, ed., *The Popular and Critical Bible Encyclopedia and Scriptural Dictionary*. Chicago, Severance, 1910. 3 vols., 600 maps and engravings.

Grueber, H. A., *Coins of the Roman Republic in the British Museum*. 3 vols. London, British Museum, 1910. Illustrated.

Halliday, Garnet R., *Money Talks About the Bible*. Hollywood, Calif., Halliday, 1948. 28 pp.; 59 illustrations.

Hastings, James, *A Dictionary of the Bible*. New York, Scribner, 1903. 5 vols., illustrated. See section on "Money."

————, *A Dictionary of Christ and the Gospels*. New York, Scribner, 1908. 2 vols. See "Money."

BIBLIOGRAPHY   171

Head, Barclay V., *Historia Numorum* (A Manual of Greek Numismatics). London, Milford, 1911. 964–lxxxvii pp.; illustrated.
Helps to the Study of the Bible. London, Oxford University Press, undated. Illustrated.
Hill, George Francis, volume on *Palestine* in *A Catalogue of Greek Coins in the British Museum.* London, British Museum, 1914. Illustrated.
Josephus, Flavius, *Works* (translated by William Whiston). Philadelphia, McKay, undated. 978 pp.
Klawans, Zander H., *Reading and Dating Roman Imperial Coins.* Racine, Wis., Whitman, 1953. Illustrated.
Madden, Frederic W., *History of Jewish Coinage.* London, Quaritch, 1864. 339–xi pp.; 254 woodcuts of coins.
Mattingly and Sydenham, *The Roman Imperial Coinage,* Vols. I and II. London, Spink & Son, 1923; reprinted 1948. Illustrated.
McCabe, James D., *The Pictorial History of the World.* Philadelphia, National Publishing Co., 1878. 1342 pp.; illustrated.
McClintock and Strong, *Cyclopedia of Biblical, Theological, and Ecclesiastical Literature.* New York, Harper, 1889. 12 vols.; illustrated.
Milne, J. G., *Greek and Roman Coins and the Study of History.* London, Methuen, 1939. 128 pp.; 122 coin illustrations.
Murray, Alexander S., *Manual of Mythology.* New York, Scribner, Armstrong, 1874. 368 pp.; 45 plates.
Prime, William C., *Money of the Bible.* New York, Elder Numismatic Press, undated, 22 pp.
Rawlings, Gertrude Burford, *Coins and How to Know Them.* New York, Stokes, undated. 374 pp.; 206 illustrations.
Rogers, E., *A Handy Guide to Jewish Coins.* London, Spink & Son, 1914. 108 pp.; 136 coin photographs.
Romanoff, Paul, *Jewish Symbols on Ancient Jewish Coins.* Philadelphia, Jewish Publication Society, 1944.
Ward, John, *Greek Coins and Their Parent Cities.* London, Murray, 1902. 464–xxi pp.; illustrated.
Wells, H. G., *The Outline of History.* New York, The Macmillan Company, 1929. 1324 pp.; illustrated.

Appendix 3

NUMISMATIC KIT

To demonstrate the way in which very ancient money was made collectors may enjoy using a small illustrative kit containing:

1. *A die.* The bottom of an ordinary tin can (the end of the can which is marked with indented figures and letters) makes an excellent die. It will look more realistic if it is trimmed down to a small square or circle.
2. *A small mallet.*
3. *A punch.* The moneyer's punch was of strong metal, of course, but for demonstration purposes one made of wood is adequate. A good punch can be made from the handle of a dishmop, ice-pick, or other kitchen gadget. This should be cut straight across the lower end, then the end should be trimmed so that it has a projecting square not over a sixteenth of an inch deep.
4. *Modeling clay* of the type which can be bought at toy stores or ten-cent stores.

Pinch off a piece of modeling clay the size of a small marble. Roll it in your palm until it is very pliable. This is now your flan. Lay the flan on the figures or letters of your die. Level the punch on the flan. Strike the punch with your mallet. You have a clay coin. Perhaps it is even slightly cracked on the edges, as are many ancient coins.

Index

SELECTED
BIBLIOGRAPHY

Akerman, J. Y., Numismatic Illustrations Of The Narrative Portions Of
    The New Testament
Banks, F. A., Coins Of The Bible Days
Bellinger, A., Essays On The Coins Of Alexander The Great
Bellinger, A., Syrian Tetradrachms
Ben-Ali, A., Ships And Parts Of Ships On Ancient Coins
Casson, L. & Price, M., Coins, Culture And History In The Ancient
    World
Cunningham, A., Coins Of Alexander's Successors In The East
Forrer, L., The Weber Collection Of Greek Coins (3 Volumes)
Grant, M., Ancient History Atlas
Grose, S. W., The McClean Collection Of Greek Coins (3 Volumes)
Head, B. V., Historia Numorum
Hendlin, D., A Guide To Ancient Jewish Coinage
Hill, G. F., Descriptive Catalog Of Ancient Jewish Coinage
Hill, P. V., The Dating And Arrangement Of The Undated Coins Of
    Rome A.D. 98–148
Icard, S., Dictionary Of Greek Coin Inscriptions
Jameson, R., Monnaies Greques Antiques Et Imperiales, Romaines (4
    Volumes)
Kindler, A., Coins Of The Land Of Israel
Klawans, Z. H., Outline Of Ancient Greek Coins
Klawans, Z. H., Reading And Dating Roman Imperial Coins
Klutznik Museum, Grossman Collection Of Ancient Judean Coins
Mattson, G. O., The Gods, Godesses And Heros On The Ancient Coins
    Of Bible Lands
Mattingly, H. A., Catalog Of Coins Of The Roman Empire In The
    British Museum
Mattingly, H. A., Roman Coins
Mayer, L. A., A Bibliography Of Jewish Numismatics
Meshorer, Y., Coins Of The Second Temple Period
Meshorer, Y., History Of Nabatean Coins
Meshorer, Y., Sylloge Numorum Graecorum—Volume VI—Palestine
Milne, J. G., Catalog Of Alexandrian Coins

Newell, E. T., Coinages Of The Eastern Seleucid Mints
Newell, E. T., Coinages Of The Western Seleucid Mints
Newell, E. T., Standard Ptolemaic Silver
Plante, R., Greek Coin Types And Their Identification
Plante, R., Greek, Semitic, Asiatic Coins And How To Read Them
Price, M., Coins And The Bible
Price, M. J. & Trell, B. L., Coins And Their Cities
Reece, R., Roman Coins
Reifenberg, A. Ancient Jewish Coinage
Reinach, T., Jewish Coins
Rodewald, C., Money In The Age Of Tiberius
Rogers, E., Handy Guide To Jewish Coins
Romanoff, P., Jewish Symbols On Ancient Jewish Coins
Rosenberger, M., Collection Of Ancient Coins Of Israel (4 Volumes)
Rynearson, P. F., Byzantine Coins And Values
Schalit, A., World History Of The Jewish People, The Hellenistic Age
Seaby, H. A., Roman Silver Coins (4 Volumes)
Sear, D., Roman Coins And Their Values
Sear, D., Byzantine Coins And Their Values
Sear, D., Greek Coins And Their Values (2 Volumes)
Sear, D., Greek Imperial Coinage
Seltman, C., Greek Coins
Sheppart T. & Musham, J. F., Money, Scales And Weights
Smith, W., Classical Dictionary Of Biography, Mythology And
          Geography
Sperber, D. Roman Palestine 200–400 Money And Prices
Stevenson, S. W., Dictionary Of Roman Coins
Sutherland, C. H. V., Coinage Of The Roman Imperial Policy
Sutherland, C. H. V., The Emperor And The Coinage
Sutherland, C. H. V., & Carson, R., Roman Imperial Coinage
                          (11 Volumes)
Sydenham, E., The Coinage of Ceaseria In Cappadocia
Sydenham, E., Coinage Of Nero
Westdal, S. Dictionary Of Roman Coin Inscriptions
Williamson, G. C., The Money Of The Bible
Wirgin, W. & Mandel, S., The History Of Coins And Symbols Of Ancient
                          Isreal
Yonah, M. A. & Bara, A., World History Of The Jewish People, The
                          Herodian Period

DURST PUBLICATIONS
RELATING TO ANCIENT NUMISMATICS

SYMBOLISM ON GREEK COINS
Baldwin, Agnes

A thorough study which appeared in the American Journal of Numismatics and which lends insight and pleasure to the collection and understanding of the Ancient coins of Greece. Profusely illustrated. 128 pages, 7" x 10". Reprint of 1914 edition.
ISBN 0-915262-10-X   **$16.50**

ESSAYS ON THE COINAGE OF ALEXANDER THE GREAT
Bellinger, Alfred R.

Considered a major reference on the social, political and economic factors in the times of Alexander the Great. By a major scholar. Has sold for $185 on the secondary market. Originally a Numismatic Study issued by the American Numismatic Society in 1963. Chapters include the Kings Money; the Kings Finances; the Successors and the Cites; the Sequel of Events; a major bibliography and 3 plates. 145 pages, 7" x 10". Limited edition of 500 of this reprint. Reprint of 1962 edition.
ISBN 0-915262-33-9   **$30.00**

SYRIAN TETRADRACHMS
Bellinger, Alfred R.

The significant study by a major scholar on the coinage of the Romans during their occupation of Syria. Historically important. 116 pp., plus 26 plates illustrating hundreds of coins. Rerint of 1940 edition.
ISBN 0-915262-57-6   **$26.00**

TROY THE COINS
Bellinger, Alfred R.

The only major work on the coins of Illium (Troy), by a known scholar. Now commands well over $100 for an original copy. Originally published by an important University Press. 288 pages, 7" x10", including 54 pages of outstanding coin photo plates. Only 500 numbered copies of this reprint of 1961 edition.
ISBN 0-915262-32-0   **$35.00**

ANCIENT HISTORY ATLAS
Grant, Michael

A marvelous book of maps, by a recognized scholar, providing those interested in Classical history and numismatics with details on long lost communities, trade routes, centers of religion, etc., from 1700 B.C. to 500 A.D. 128 pp., ill., soft. Reprint of 1971 edition.
ISBN 0-915262-73-8   **$10.00**

DICTIONARY OF GREEK COIN INSCRIPTIONS
Icard, Severin

The only complete dictionary of Greek coin inscriptions of antiquity, including partial inscriptions, abbreviations, etc. A major work originally published in Europe in the early twentieth century. Easy to use. Complete instructions are included in English. 600 pages, 7" x 10". Reprint limited edition, 500 copies.
ISBN 0-915262-31-2   **42.50**

THE MEDALS OF GIOVANNI CAVINO - THE PADUAN
Laurence, Richard H.

A famous series of medallic reproductions of Roman Coins, produced by "The Paduan" in the 1600's are catalogued here. The medals are prized collectibles, which can fool the collector of Roman coins. This book helps to identify and classifies the reproductions. 32 pp., ill., soft. Reprint of 1881 edition.
ISBN 0-915262-56-8   **$5.00**

STANDARD PTOLEMAIC SILVER
Newell, Edward T.

The basic reference on the Greek Ptolemaic Dynasty in Egypt, post Alexander the Great. Heavily illustrated, new reattribution supplement and value guide. 32 pp., soft.
ISBN   0-915262-49-5   **$6.00**

HANDY GUIDE TO JEWISH COINS
Rogers, Rev. Edgar, M.A.

A reprint of a most thorough and respected study of Ancient Judeaic coins, with many excellent plates, illustrating the coinage. Now a sought after and costly book. 128 pages, 6" x 9". Limited edition reprint of 1915 edition.
ISBN   0-915262-14-2   **$13.50**

ATHENIAN COINAGE
Starr, Chester

The major reference on this most popular collecting area of Ancient Greek Coinage. A detailed, historical and numismatic treatise, originally published by prestigious Oxford University. 128 pp., 26 pl. Reprint of 1970 edition.
ISBN   0-915262-55-X   **$20.00**

COINAGE OF THE ROMAN IMPERIAL POLICY
Sutherland, C.H.V.

A classic book thoroughly covering the coinage of Rome from the end of the Roman Republic (30 BC) to the creation of the Roman Empire (67 AD). The period starts with Augustus and ends with Nero, a time of great tumult and change in the Roman World (See also Coinage of the Roman Republic (300 BC-30 BC) the major reference on numismatics of the period just prior to Roman Imperial times which we have reprinted). The author is a respected scholar. Heavily illustrated with 17 full page plates. 250 pages, 6" x 9". Reprint of 1952 edition.
ISBN   0-15262-19-3   **$25.00**

THE COINAGE OF NERO
Sydenham, Edward

The only study of the coinage of this popular and most collectible series of Roman Coins, well written and illustrated. 192 pp. Reprint of 1920 edition.
ISBN   0-915262-04-5   **$30.00**

THE COINAGE OF THE ROMAN REPUBLIC
Sydenham, Edward

The standard reference on the subject which is the extensive numismatic issuance of Roman Coins from 300 B.C.-30 B.C. Substantial plates, long out-of-print, and originals subject to high price bids at book auctions. 400 pages, 6" x 9". Reprint of 1952 edition.
ISBN   0-915262-04-5   **$30.00**

DICTIONARY OF ROMAN COIN INSCRIPTIONS
Westdal, Stewart

A thorough listing of the thousands of inscriptions on Roman and Roman Colonial coin issues. Provides ability to identify coinage as to location and ruler, most important in a field where coins are often poorly or un-identified. Includes so-called Greek Imperial (Roman Colonial) issues, and Indices of rulers and geographical locations. New expanded 4th edition. 144 pp., soft.
ISBN   0-915262-72-X   **$10.00**